Hands-On Function Programming with TypeScript

Explore functional and reactive programming to create robust and testable TypeScript applications

Remo H. Jansen

BIRMINGHAM - MUMBAI

Hands-On Functional Programming with TypeScript

Commissioning Editor: Richa Tripathi
Acquisition Editor: Denim Pinto
Content Development Editor: Anugraha Arunagiri
Technical Editor: Ashi Singh
Copy Editor: Safis Editing
Project Coordinator: Ulhas Kambali
Proofreader: Safis Editing
Indexer: Rekha Nair
Graphics: Tom Scaria
Production Coordinator: Saili Kale

First published: January 2019

Production reference: 1290119

Published by Packt Publishing Ltd.
Livery Place
35 Livery Street
Birmingham
B3 2PB, UK.

ISBN 978-1-78883-143-7

www.packtpub.com

To Lorraine, for being my sword in my victories and my shield in my defeats. Without your support, I wouldn't be where I am and I wouldn't be the person I am today. Thank you!

– Remo H. Jansen

`mapt.io`

Mapt is an online digital library that gives you full access to over 5,000 books and videos, as well as industry leading tools to help you plan your personal development and advance your career. For more information, please visit our website.

Why subscribe?

- Spend less time learning and more time coding with practical eBooks and Videos from over 4,000 industry professionals

- Improve your learning with Skill Plans built especially for you

- Get a free eBook or video every month

- Mapt is fully searchable

- Copy and paste, print, and bookmark content

Packt.com

Did you know that Packt offers eBook versions of every book published, with PDF and ePub files available? You can upgrade to the eBook version at `www.packt.com` and as a print book customer, you are entitled to a discount on the eBook copy. Get in touch with us at `customercare@packtpub.com` for more details.

At `www.packt.com`, you can also read a collection of free technical articles, sign up for a range of free newsletters, and receive exclusive discounts and offers on Packt books and eBooks.

Foreword

When TypeScript was officially announced on October 1, 2012, the only docs available was the dense official language specification. It was not easily accessible to beginner developers as there was significant focus on syntax. Additionally, it assumed an existing intimate knowledge of JavaScript. Nevertheless, it was complete in terms of TypeScript features at the time, and JavaScript was not as feature-rich as it is today. So, it was a plausible entry point into TypeScript, and that is what I and many others at the time used to learn TypeScript.

How times have changed. Over time, TypeScript has gained a number of features, and so has JavaScript. Keeping up to date now means following relevant GitHub issues and pull requests on Microsoft/TypeScript and reading up on the understanding offered by key developers. Remo is one of those key developers. I got introduced to Remo through his insightful comments on TypeScript issues and then discovered his blog (`blog.wolksoftware.com`). Remo's blog has been a great help in dissecting important features such as JavaScript decorators and explaining how they are implemented in TypeScript. I find myself linking fellow developers to his docs instead of the alternatives due to the high quality of his work.

Not only has Remo been a great help in understanding TypeScript (and JavaScript), but he has also been a great asset to the TypeScript library ecosystem. One question that I commonly receive from developers is how to do dependency injection in TypeScript. My answer is always a direct link to Remo's extremely useful InversifyJS library (`inversify.io`).

One of the key concerns that uninformed developers have had about TypeScript is "it only supports object-oriented programming." That is simply not true. TypeScript supports all JavaScript paradigms, and functional programming has first-class support. In fact, it provides a vital piece of famous functional programming languages (compile-time type information) for JavaScript developers.

All programming tasks can be considered as simple (data plus data transformation). This is the mental model encouraged by functional programming aficionados. To have a deep understanding of functional programs as a data transform pipeline, you need a way to define your data structures. This is what is only provided by TypeScript. In the absence of TypeScript, you see various (somewhat arbitrary) syntax elements used to describe the data structures that are flowing through your functional programs.

So, if you want to do world-class functional programming and your programming environment forces you (if only by convenience) to use JavaScript, please consider TypeScript and know that you are not alone. Remo H. Jansen is here to help you.

Basarat Ali Syed

Microsoft MVP and one of the leading global references of the TypeScript community.

Contributors

About the author

Remo H. Jansen lives in Dublin, Ireland, where he works as the managing director of Wolk Software Limited and as a part-time lecturer at CCT College Dublin. Remo is a Microsoft MVP and an active member of the TypeScript community. He is the author of *Learning TypeScript 2.x*, organizes the Dublin TypeScript and Dublin OSS meetups, writes a blog, and maintains some open source projects on GitHub. Remo is available for conference talks, independent consulting, and corporate training services opportunities.

Thanks to everyone who participated in this book for your support and hard work: my friends, Lorraine, and my family, for your support and patience, and to the TypeScript teams and its contributors for creating what has become my favorite programming language.

About the reviewers

Gaurav Aroraa has an M.Phil in computer science. He is a Microsoft MVP, a lifetime member of Computer Society of India (CSI), an advisory member of IndiaMentor, certified as a Scrum trainer/coach, XEN for ITIL-F, and APMG for PRINCE-F and PRINCE-P. He is an open source developer, a contributor to TechNet Wiki, and the founder of Ovatic Systems Private Limited. In the more than 20 years of his career, he has mentored thousands of students and industry professionals. You can tweet Gaurav using his Twitter handle, @g_arora.

To my wife, Shuby Arora, and my angel (daughter), Aarchi Arora, who permitted me to steal time for this book from the time I was supposed to spend with them. Thanks to the entire Packt team, especially Ulhas and Anugraha Arunagiri, whose coordination and communication during the period was tremendous, and Denim Pinto, who introduced me for this book.

Sergio Pacheco Jimenez is a Software engineer residing in Seville, Spain. He is mainly focused on .NET, JavaScript and web development. For the last few years, he has been using and advocating TypeScript. Currently, he is working on the banking industry.

Packt is searching for authors like you

If you're interested in becoming an author for Packt, please visit authors.packtpub.com and apply today. We have worked with thousands of developers and tech professionals, just like you, to help them share their insight with the global tech community. You can make a general application, apply for a specific hot topic that we are recruiting an author for, or submit your own idea.

Table of Contents

Preface   1

Chapter 1: Functional Programming Fundamentals   9
    Is TypeScript a functional programming language?   9
    The benefits of functional programming   10
    Introducing functional programming   11
    Pure functions   12
    side-effects   13
    Referential transparency   16
    Stateless versus stateful   16
    Declarative versus imperative programming   17
    Immutability   19
    Functions as first-class citizens   21
    Lambda expressions   22
    Function arity   23
    Higher-order functions   23
    Laziness   24
    Summary   26

Chapter 2: Mastering Functions   27
    Function types   28
        Named and anonymous functions   29
        Function declarations and function expressions   31
    Working with function parameters   32
        Trailing commas in function arguments   32
        Functions with optional parameters   33
        Functions with default parameters   34
        Functions with rest parameters   35
        Function overloading   38
        Specialized overloading signature   40
    Function scope and hoisting   40
    Immediately-invoked functions   44
    Tag functions and tagged templates   48
    Summary   49

Chapter 3: Mastering Asynchronous Programming   51
    Callbacks and higher-order functions   51
        Arrow functions   52
    Callback hell   54

Promises   56
Covariant checking in callback parameters   61
Generators   62
Asynchronous functions – async and await   64
Asynchronous generators   66
Asynchronous iteration (for await...of)   67
Delegating to another generator (yield*)   68
Summary   69

Chapter 4: The Runtime – The Event Loop and the this Operator 71
The environment   72
Understanding the event loop   73
Frames   73
Stack   75
Queue   75
Heap   75
The event loop   75
The this operator   76
The this operator in the global context   77
The this operator in the function context   77
The call, apply, and bind methods   79
Summary   83

Chapter 5: The Runtime – Closures and Prototypes   85
Prototypes   85
Instance properties versus class properties   87
Prototypal inheritance   90
Prototype chains and property shadowing   94
Accessing the prototype of an object   96
Closures   96
Static variables powered by closures   98
Private members powered by closures   101
Summary   103

Chapter 6: Functional Programming Techniques   105
Composition techniques   106
Composition   106
Partial application   108
Currying   110
strictBindCallApply   112
Pipes   112
Other techniques   114
Point-free style   114
Recursion   116
Pattern matching   117
Summary   118

Chapter 7: Category Theory   119
  Category theory   119
  Functors   121
    Applicative   122
    Maybe   123
    Either   126
    Monads   129
  Summary   131

Chapter 8: Immutability, Optics, and Laziness   133
  Immutability   133
  Optics   136
    Lenses   137
    Prisms   141
  Laziness   144
  Summary   147

Chapter 9: Functional-Reactive Programming   149
  Reactive programming   149
    Functional programming versus functional-reactive programming   150
    The benefits of functional-reactive programming   150
  Working with observables   150
    The observer pattern   151
    The iterator pattern   152
    Creating observables   153
      Creating observables from a value   153
      Creating observables from arrays   154
      Creating observables from events   156
      Creating observables from callbacks   156
      Creating observables from promises   157
    Cold and hot observables   158
  Working with operators   159
    Pipe   159
    Max   159
    Every   160
    Find   161
    Filter   161
    Map   162
    Reduce   163
    Throttle   163
    Merge   165
    Zip   165
  Summary   166

Chapter 10: Real-World Functional Programming   167
  Working with Ramda   168

Composition   168
Partial application and currying   169
Lenses   170
Working with Immutable.js   174
Working with Immer   176
Working with Funfix   177
Summary   180

Appendix A: Functional Programming Learning Road Map   181
Beginner   181
Advanced beginner   182
Intermediate   182
Proficient   183
Expert   183
Summary   184

Appendix B: Directory of TypeScript Functional Programming Libraries   185
Functional programming   186
Category theory   186
Laziness   187
Immutability   187
Optics and lenses   187
Functional-reactive programming   188
Others   188
Summary   188

Other Books You May Enjoy   189

Index   193

Preface

Functional programming is a programming paradigm that treats computation as the evaluation of mathematical functions and avoids changing-state and mutable data. The origins of the functional programming paradigm can be traced back to the 1930s when Alonzo Church introduced Lambda calculus. Lambda calculus presents a theoretical framework for describing functions and their evaluation, and is a mathematical abstraction rather than a programming language. However, Lambda calculus is the foundation of most functional programming languages.

In the late 1950s, Lisp, one of the first functional programming languages, was developed by John McCarthy. Lisp introduced many functional programming paradigm features, and it was the primary influence of other popular functional programming languages, such as Scheme and Clojure.

In 1973, Robin Milner created ML at the University of Edinburgh. ML eventually developed into several alternative languages, the most common of which are now OCaml and Standard ML. In 1977, John Backus defined functional programs in a way that allows an "algebra of programs" and follows the principle of compositionality. In 1985, Research Software Limited released Miranda, and the interest in lazy functional programming languages grew. After a couple of years, more than a dozen non-strict, purely functional programming languages existed. In 1987, at the conference on functional programming languages and computer architecture in Portland, Oregon, there was a strong consensus that a committee should be formed to define an open standard for such languages; Haskell was born.

The 1970s and 1980s were years of significant advancement for functional programming. However, during the 1990s and 2000s, functional programming lost market share against object-oriented programming languages, such as Java and C#.

In the 2010s, the adoption of JavaScript grew exponentially, and it became the most popular programming language. The Scheme programming language is one of the main influences of JavaScript and, as a result, JavaScript implements many functional programming features, such as support for higher-order functions. JavaScript became the first contact with functional programming for many young developers. However, because JavaScript is a multi-paradigm programming language, many ignored its functional programming capabilities. However, in recent times, thanks to the arrival of technologies highly influenced by functional programmings principles, such as React, RxJS, and Redux, there has been a significant increase in interest in functional programming within the JavaScript community.

As the popularity of JavaScript grew, the complexity of JavaScript applications also grew exponentially. Web user interfaces became much more sophisticated, and JavaScript started to be used in a number of alternative scenarios, such as backend applications. The TypeScript programming language was then introduced as a tool that allows us to manage the new levels of complexity.

TypeScript aims to reduce the complexity of a system by adding a static type system to JavaScript. Static type systems can be used to detect errors at compilation time as a beneficial form of in-code documentation. Static type systems can be very beneficial in functional programming. Most object-oriented programming languages, such as Java and C#, are slowly adopting functional programming features, and sophisticated static type systems are something that is many times associated with purely functional programming languages, such as Haskell.

This book is not going to encourage you to stop using object-oriented programming. Instead, we are going to try to think about both the functional programming and the object-oriented programming paradigms as two different solutions to the same problem: managing complexity:

> *"Object-oriented programming makes code understandable by encapsulating moving parts. Functional programming makes code understandable by minimizing moving parts."*

> *– Michael Feathers*

The popularity of distributed systems is increasing as the adoption of cloud computing continues to grow and, as a result, functional programming is expected to rise in popularity over the next decade because it is particularly well suited for concurrent systems and distributed systems. Functional programming encourages the implementation of stateless components, which can be scaled with ease. Since the complexity of distributed systems is usually high, this is just another example of how functional programming can be used as a weapon against complexity.

Mastering TypeScript together with the principles and techniques of both object-oriented programming and functional programming can provide us with a richer toolset to fight against complexity in our systems. This book will provide you with knowledge about a wide range of functional programming principles, patterns, and techniques that should help you to become a more versatile software engineer and prepare you for dealing with the increasing complexity in modern web applications.

Who this book is for

If you are a developer aiming to learn functional programming for the very first time and improve the quality of your applications, then this book is for you. No prior knowledge of functional programming is required. However, a basic understanding of JavaScript and TypeScript is recommended to make the most out of this book.

What this book covers

Chapter 1, *Functional Programming Fundamentals*, introduces the main functional programming terms, such as pure functions.

Chapter 2, *Mastering Functions*, takes an in-depth look at the main building block in a functional programming application—functions. The chapter also explores most of the function-related features in TypeScript. We will learn how to work with functions in many different scenarios and how to take advantage of the TypeScript type system features while working with functions.

Chapter 3, *Mastering Asynchronous Programming*, takes an in-depth look at the main asynchronous programming APIs in JavaScript and TypeScript, including callbacks, promises, generators, and asynchronous functions. These APIs are relevant in functional programming because they can be used to implement lazy evaluation.

Chapter 4, *The Runtime – The Event Loop and the this Operator*, is the first chapter of two that are dedicated to exploring concepts about the runtime that are relevant for a number of functional programming techniques. For example, we can gain a much better understanding of recursion if we understand the event loop.

Chapter 5, *The Runtime – Closures and Prototypes*, is the second chapter dedicated to exploring concepts about the runtime that are relevant to a number of functional programming techniques. For example, understanding closures can help us to understand how some higher-order functions work.

Chapter 6, *Functional Programming Techniques*, explores the main functional programming techniques and patterns in detail. We will explore concepts such as partial function application, functional composition, and currying. This chapter also explores many other functional programming techniques and patterns, such as point-free style.

Chapter 7, *Category Theory*, explores category theory. You will learn about what algebraic data types are and what the relationships between them are. You will then learn how to implement some of the main algebraic data types, including functors and monads.

Chapter 8, *Immutability, Optics, and Laziness*, explores three important functional programming techniques. You will learn about what lazy evaluation is, what its benefits are, and how to implement it. You will also learn about immutable data structures, their benefits, and how to implement them. Finally, you will learn about functional optics and how they can help with immutable data structures.

Chapter 9, *Functional-Reactive Programming*, explores the functional-reactive programming paradigm. We will learn about what observables are and how they can be used to simplify our code. We will also learn how to use RxJS, the leading reactive-programming library in the JavaScript ecosystem.

Chapter 10, *Real-World Functional Programming*, explores some production-ready functional programming libraries, such as Ramda and Funfix, to create real-world functional programming applications. \

Appendix A, *Functional Programming Learning Road Map*, this was developed for Fantasyland institute of learning for the LambdaConf conference. It is used to track our level of knowledge regarding functional programming.

Appendix B, *Directory of TypeScript Functional Programming Libraries*, In this appendix, you will find a list of functional programming libraries compatible with TypeScript grouped.

To get the most out of this book

You don't need any additional material to follow this book. No prior knowledge of functional programming is required. However, a basic understanding of JavaScript and TypeScript is recommended to make the most use of this book.

It is recommended reading the chapters in order. However, if you are new to functional programming and already have advanced knowledge of functions, asynchronous programming, and the runtime, you could maybe skip chapters two to five.

You can refer to the TypeScript handbook at `http://www.typescriptlang.org/docs/handbook/basic-types.html` if you have some experience with JavaScript, but TypeScript is new to you. This resource might be especially useful if TypeScript is your first statically typed programming language. Alternatively, you can refer to the book *Learning TypeScript 2.x, Second Edition*, also by *Remo H. Jansen* and *Packt Publishing*.

If you need help installing Node.js, you can refer to the official documentation at `https://nodejs.org/en/download/package-manager`. If you need help installing TypeScript, you can refer to the official documentation at `http://www.typescriptlang.org/docs/handbook/typescript-in-5-minutes.html`.

Download the example code files

You can download the example code files for this book from your account at
`www.packt.com`. If you purchased this book elsewhere, you can visit
`www.packt.com/support` and register to have the files emailed directly to you.

You can download the code files by following these steps:

1. Log in or register at `www.packt.com`.
2. Select the **SUPPORT** tab.
3. Click on **Code Downloads & Errata**.
4. Enter the name of the book in the **Search** box and follow the onscreen instructions.

Once the file is downloaded, please make sure that you unzip or extract the folder using the latest version of:

- WinRAR/7-Zip for Windows
- Zipeg/iZip/UnRarX for Mac
- 7-Zip/PeaZip for Linux

The code bundle for the book is also hosted on GitHub at `https://github.com/PacktPublishing/Hands-On-Functional-Programming-with-Typescript`. In case there's an update to the code, it will be updated on the existing GitHub repository.

We also have other code bundles from our rich catalog of books and videos available at `https://github.com/PacktPublishing/`. Check them out!

Download the color images

We also provide a PDF file that has color images of the screenshots/diagrams used in this book. You can download it here: `https://www.packtpub.com/sites/default/files/downloads/9781788831437_ColorImages.pdf`.

Conventions used

There are a number of text conventions used throughout this book.

`CodeInText`: Indicates code words in text, database table names, folder names, filenames, file extensions, pathnames, dummy URLs, user input, and Twitter handles. Here is an example: "Mount the downloaded `WebStorm-10*.dmg` disk image file as another disk in your system."

A block of code is set as follows:

```
function find<T>(arr: T[], filter: (i: T) => boolean) {
    return arr.filter(filter);
}

find(heroes, (h) => h.name === "Spiderman");
```

When we wish to draw your attention to a particular part of a code block, the relevant lines or items are set in bold:

```
const valueOfThis = { name: "Anakin", surname: "Skywalker" };
const greet = person.greet.bind(valueOfThis);
greet.call(valueOfThis, "Mos espa", "Tatooine");
greet.apply(valueOfThis, ["Mos espa", "Tatooine"]);
// Hi, my name is Remo Jansen. I'm from Mos espa Tatooine.
```

Any command-line input or output is written as follows:

```
npm install ramda @types/ramda
```

Bold: Indicates a new term, an important word, or words that you see on screen. For example, words in menus or dialog boxes appear in the text like this. Here is an example: "Select **System info** from the **Administration** panel."

Warnings or important notes appear like this.

Tips and tricks appear like this.

Get in touch

Feedback from our readers is always welcome.

General feedback: If you have questions about any aspect of this book, mention the book title in the subject of your message and email us at customercare@packtpub.com.

Errata: Although we have taken every care to ensure the accuracy of our content, mistakes do happen. If you have found a mistake in this book, we would be grateful if you would report this to us. Please visit www.packt.com/submit-errata, selecting your book, clicking on the Errata Submission Form link, and entering the details.

Piracy: If you come across any illegal copies of our works in any form on the Internet, we would be grateful if you would provide us with the location address or website name. Please contact us at copyright@packt.com with a link to the material.

If you are interested in becoming an author: If there is a topic that you have expertise in, and you are interested in either writing or contributing to a book, please visit authors.packtpub.com.

Reviews

Please leave a review. Once you have read and used this book, why not leave a review on the site that you purchased it from? Potential readers can then see and use your unbiased opinion to make purchase decisions, we at Packt can understand what you think about our products, and our authors can see your feedback on their book. Thank you!

For more information about Packt, please visit packt.com.

1
Functional Programming Fundamentals

JavaScript has been a multi-paradigm programming language since its inception back in 1995. It allows us to take advantage of an **object-oriented programming (OOP)** style along with a functional programming style. The same can be said of TypeScript. However, for functional programming, TypeScript is even better suited than JavaScript because, as we will learn in this chapter, static type systems and type inference are both very important features in functional programming languages such as the ML family of programming languages, for example.

The JavaScript and TypeScript ecosystems have experienced a significant increase in interest in functional programming over the last few years. I believe that this increase in interest can be attributed to the success of React. React is a library developed by Facebook for building user interfaces, and it is highly influenced by some core functional programming concepts.

In this chapter, we will focus on learning some of the most basic functional programming concepts and principles.

In this chapter, you will learn about the following:

- The main characteristics of functional programming
- The main benefits of functional programming
- Pure functions
- side-effects
- Immutability
- Function arity
- Higher-order functions
- Laziness

Is TypeScript a functional programming language?

The answer to this question is yes, but only in part. TypeScript is a multi-paradigm programming language and, as a result, it includes many influences from both OOP languages and functional programming paradigms.

However, if we focus on TypeScript as a functional programming language, we can observe that it is not a purely functional programming language because, for example, the TypeScript compiler doesn't force our code to be free of side-effects.

Not being a purely functional programming language should not be interpreted as something negative. TypeScript provides us with an extensive set of features that allow us to take advantage of some of the best features of the world of OOP languages and the world of functional programming languages. This has allowed TypeScript-type systems to attain a very good compromise between productivity and formality.

The benefits of functional programming

Writing TypeScript code using a functional programming style has many benefits, among which we can highlight the following:

- **Our code is testable:** If we try to write our functions as pure functions, we will be able to write unit tests extremely easily. We will learn more about pure functions later in this chapter.
- **Our code is easy to reason about:** Functional programming can seem hard to understand for developers with a lack of experience in functional programming. However, when an application is implemented correctly using the functional programming paradigm, the results are very small functions (often one-line functions) and very declarative APIs that can be reasoned about with ease. Also, pure functions only work with their arguments, which means that when we want to understand what a function does, we only need to examine the function itself and we don't need to be concerned about any other external variables.

- **Concurrency:** Most of our functions are stateless, and our code is mostly stateless. We push state out of the core of our application, which makes our applications much more likely to be able to support many concurrent operations and it will be more scalable. We will learn more about stateless code later in this chapter.
- **Simpler caching:** Caching strategies to cache results become much simpler when we can predict the output of a function given its arguments.

Introducing functional programming

Functional programming (**FP**) is a programming paradigm that receives its name from the way we build applications when we use it. In a programming paradigm such as OOP, the main building blocks that we use to create an application are objects (objects are declared using classes). However, in FP, we use functions as the main building block in our applications.

Each new programming paradigm introduces a series of concepts and ideas associated with it. Some of these concepts are universal and are also of interest while learning a different programming paradigm. In OOP, we have concepts such as inheritance, encapsulation, and polymorphism. In functional programming, concepts include higher-order functions, function partial application, immutability, and referential transparency. We are going to examine some of these concepts in this chapter.

Michael Feathers, the author of the SOLID acronym and many other well-known software engineering principles, once wrote the following:

> *"Object-oriented programming makes code understandable by encapsulating moving parts. Functional programming makes code understandable by minimizing moving parts."*

– Michael Feathers

The preceding quote mentions moving parts. We should understand these moving parts as **state changes** (also known as **state mutations**). In OOP, we use encapsulation to prevent objects from being aware of the state mutations of other objects. In functional programming, we try to avoid dealing with state mutations instead of encapsulating them.

FP reduces the number of places in which state changes take place within an application and tries to move these places into the boundaries of the application to try to keep the application's core stateless.

A mutable state is bad because it makes the behavior of our code harder to predict. Take the following function, for example:

```
function isIndexPage() {
   return window.location.pathname === "/";
}
```

The preceding code snippet declared a function named `isIndexPage`. This function can be used to check whether the current page is the root page in a web application based on the current path.

The path is some data that changes all the time, so we can consider it a piece of state. If we try to predict the result of invoking the `isIndexPage`, we will need to know the current state. The problem is that we could wrongly assume that the state has not changed since the last known state. We can solve this problem by transforming the preceding function into what is known in FP as a **pure function**, as we will learn in the following section.

Pure functions

FP introduces a number of concepts and principles that will help us to improve the predictability of our code. In this section, we are going to learn about one of these core concepts—pure functions.

A function can be considered pure when it returns a value that is computed using only the arguments passed to it. Also, a pure function avoids mutating its arguments or any other external variables. As a result, a pure function always returns the same value given the same arguments, independently of when it is invoked.

The `isIndexPage` function declared in the preceding section is not a pure function because it accesses the `pathname` variable, which has not been passed as an argument to the function. We can transform the preceding function into a pure function by rewriting it as follows:

```
function isIndexPage(pathname: string) {
   return pathname === "/";
}
```

Even though this is a basic example, we can easily perceive that the newer version is much easier to predict. Pure functions help us to make our code easier to understand, maintain, and test.

Imagine that we wanted to write a unit test for the impure version of the `isIndexPage` function. We would encounter some problems when trying to write a test because the function uses the `window.location` object. We could overcome this issue by using a mocking framework, but it would add a lot of complexity to our unit tests just because we didn't use a pure function.

On the other hand, testing the pure version of the `isIndexPage` function would be straightforward, as follows:

```
function shouldReturnTrueWhenPathIsIndex(){
    let expected = true;
    let result = isIndexPage("/");
    if (expected !== result) {
        throw new Error('Expected ${expected} to equals ${result}');
    }
}

function shouldReturnFalseWhenPathIsNotIndex() {
    let expected = false;
    let result = isIndexPage("/someotherpage");
    if (expected !== result) {
        throw new Error('Expected ${expected} to equals ${result}');
    }
}
```

Now that we understand how functional programming helps us to write better code by avoiding state mutations, we can learn about side-effects and referential transparency.

side-effects

In the preceding section, we learned that a pure function returns a value that can be computed using only the arguments passed to it. A pure function also avoids mutating its arguments or any other external variable that is not passed to the function as an argument. In FP terminology, it is common to say that a pure function is a function that has no side-effects, which means that, when we invoke a pure function, we can expect that the function is not going to interfere (through a state mutation) with any other component in our application.

Certain programming languages, such as Haskell, can ensure that an application is free of side-effects using their type system. TypeScript has fantastic interoperability with JavaScript, but the downside of this, compared to a more isolated language such as Haskell, is that the type system is not able to guarantee that our application is free from side-effects. However, we can use some FP techniques to improve the type safety of our TypeScript applications. Let's take a look at an example:

```typescript
interface User {
    ageInMonths: number;
    name: string;
}

function findUserAgeByName(users: User[], name: string): number {
    if (users.length == 0) {
        throw new Error("There are no users!");
    }
    const user = users.find(u => u.name === name);
    if (!user) {
        throw new Error("User not found!");
    } else {
        return user.ageInMonths;
    }
}
```

The preceding function returns a `number`. The code compiles without issues. The problem is that the function does not always return a `number`. As a result, we can consume the function as follows and our code will compile and throw an exception at runtime:

```typescript
const users = [
    { ageInMonths: 1, name: "Remo" },
    { ageInMonths: 2, name: "Leo" }
];

// The variable userAge1 is as number
const userAge1 = findUserAgeByName(users, "Remo");
console.log('Remo is ${userAge1 / 12} years old!');

// The variable userAge2 is a number but the function throws!
const userAge2 = findUserAgeByName([], "Leo"); // Error
console.log('Leo is ${userAge2 / 12} years old!');
```

The following example showcases a new implementation of the preceding function. This time, instead of returning a number, we will explicitly return a promise. The promise forces us to then use the handler. This handler is only executed if the promise is fulfilled, which means that if the function returns an error, we will never try to convert the age to years:

```
function safeFindUserAgeByName(users: User[], name: string):
Promise<number> {
    if (users.length == 0) {
        return Promise.reject(new Error("There are no users!"));
    }
    const user = users.find(u => u.name === name);
    if (!user) {
        return Promise.reject(new Error("User not found!"));
    } else {
        return Promise.resolve(user.ageInMonths);
    }
}

safeFindUserAgeByName(users, "Remo")
    .then(userAge1 => console.log('Remo is ${userAge1 / 12} years old!'));

safeFindUserAgeByName([], "Leo") // Error
    .then(userAge1 => console.log('Leo is ${userAge1 / 12} years old!'));
```

The `Promise` type helps us to prevent errors because it expresses potential errors in an explicit way. In programming languages such as Haskell, this is the default behavior of the type system, but, in programming languages such as TypeScript, it is up to us to use types in a safer way.

We will learn more about Promises in `Chapter 3`, *Mastering Asynchronous Programming*. We will also learn more about how we can use a number of libraries to reduce the chances of side-effects in our TypeScript applications in `Chapter 8`, *Category Theory*.

If you find the idea of your JavaScript applications being free of side-effects attractive, you can try open-source projects such as `https://github.com/bodil/eslint-config-cleanjs`. This project is an ESLint configuration that aims to restrict you to a subset of JavaScript, which would be as close to an idealized pure functional language as possible. Unfortunately, at the time of publication, no similar tools are available that are specifically designed for TypeScript.

Referential transparency

Referential transparency is another concept closely related to pure functions and side-effects. A function is pure when it is free from side-effects. An expression is said to be referentially transparent when it can be replaced with its corresponding value without changing the application's behavior. For example, if we are using the following in our code:

```
let result = isIndexPage("/");
```

We know that the isIndexPage function is referentially transparent because it would be safe to substitute it for its return type. In this case, we know that when we invoke the isIndexPage function with / as an argument, the function will always return true, which means that it would be safe to do the following:

```
let result = true;
```

A pure function is a referentially transparent expression. An expression that is not referentially transparent is known as referentially opaque.

Stateless versus stateful

Pure functions and referentially transparent expressions are stateless. A piece of code is stateless when its outcomes are not influenced by previous events. For example, the results of the isIndexPage function will not be influenced by the number of times that we invoke it, or by the moment in time when we invoke it.

The opposite of stateless code is stateful code. Stateless code is very difficult to test and becomes a problem when we are trying to implement scalable and resilient systems. Resilient systems are systems that can handle server failures; there is usually more than one instance of a service, and if one of them crashes, others can continue handling traffic. Also, new instances are created automatically after one of the instances has crashed. This becomes very difficult if our servers are stateful because we need to save the current state before a crash and restore the state before we spin up a new instance. The whole process becomes much simpler when we design our servers to be stateless.

With the arrival of the cloud computing revolution, these kinds of system have become more common, and this has led to an interest in functional programming languages and design principles because functional programming encourages us to write stateless code. The opposite can be said of OOP because classes are the main construct in OOP applications. Classes encapsulate state properties that are then modified by methods, which encourages methods to be stateful and not pure.

Declarative versus imperative programming

The advocates of the FP paradigm often use declarative programming as one of its main benefits. Declarative programming is not necessarily exclusive to functional programming, but FP certainly encourages or facilitates this programming style. Before we take a look at some examples, we are going to define declarative programming and imperative programming:

- **Imperative programming** is a programming paradigm that uses statements that change a program's state. In much the same way that the imperative mood in natural languages expresses commands, an imperative program consists of commands for the computer to perform. Imperative programming focuses on describing how a program operates.
- **Declarative programming** is a programming paradigm that expresses the logic of a computation without describing its control flow. Many languages that apply this style attempt to minimize or eliminate side-effects by describing what the program must accomplish in terms of the problem domain, rather than describing how to accomplish it as a sequence of steps.

The following example calculates the average result of an exam given a collection of objects that contains an ID and a result for a list of students. This example uses an imperative programming style because, as we can see, it uses control flow statements (`for`). The example is also clearly imperative because it mutates a state. The `total` variable is declared using the `let` keyword because it is mutated as many times as results are contained in the `results` array:

```
interface Result {
 id: number;
 result:number;
}

const results: Result[] = [
 { id: 1, result: 64 },
 { id: 2, result: 87 },
 { id: 3, result: 89 }
];

function avg(arr: Result[]) {
 let total = 0;
 for (var i = 0; i < arr.length; i++) {
 total += arr[i].result;
 }
 return total / arr.length;
}
```

```
const resultsAvg = avg(results);
console.log(resultsAvg);
```

On the other hand, the following example is declarative because there are no control flow statements and there are no state mutations:

```
interface Result {
    id: number;
    result:number;
}

const results: Result[] = [
    { id: 1, result: 64 },
    { id: 2, result: 87 },
    { id: 3, result: 89 }
];

const add = (a: number, b: number) => a + b;
const division = (a: number, b: number) => a / b;

const avg = (arr: Result[]) =>
    division(arr.map(a => a.result).reduce(add, 0), arr.length)

const resultsAvg = avg(results);
console.log(resultsAvg);
```

While the previous example is declarative, it is not as declarative as it could be. The following example takes the declarative style one step further so we can get an idea of how a piece of declarative code may appear. Don't worry if you don't understand everything in this example right now. We will be able to understand it once we learn more about functional programming techniques later in this book. Note how the program is now defined as a set of very small functions that don't mutate the state and that also don't use control flow statements. These functions are reusable because they are independent of the problem that we are trying to solve. For example, the avg function can calculate an average, but it doesn't need to be an average of results:

```
const add = (a: number, b: number) => a + b;
const addMany = (...args: number[]) => args.reduce(add, 0);
const div = (a: number, b: number) => a / b;
const mapProp = <T>(k: keyof T, arr: T[]) => arr.map(a => a[k]);
const avg = (arr: number[]) => div(addMany(...arr), arr.length);

interface Result {
    id: number;
    result:number;
}
```

```
const results: Result[] = [
    { id: 1, result: 64 },
    { id: 2, result: 87 },
    { id: 3, result: 89 }
];

const resultsAvg = avg(mapProp("result", results));
console.log(resultsAvg);
```

The actual code that is specific to the problem that we are trying to solve is very small:

```
const resultsAvg = avg(mapProp("result", results));
```

This code is not reusable, but the `add`, `addMany`, `div`, `mapProp`, and `avg` functions are reusable. This demonstrates how declarative programming can lead to more reusable code than imperative programming.

Immutability

Immutability refers to the inability to change the value of a variable after a value has been assigned to it. Purely functional programming languages include immutable implementations of common data structures. For example, when we add an element to an array, we are mutating the original array. However, if we use an immutable array and we try to add a new element to it, the original array will not be mutated, and we will add the new item to a copy of it.

The following code snippet declares a class named `ImmutableList` that demonstrates how it is possible to implement an immutable array:

```
class ImmutableList<T> {
    private readonly _list: ReadonlyArray<T>;
    private _deepCloneItem(item: T) {
        return JSON.parse(JSON.stringify(item)) as T;
    }
    public constructor(initialValue?: Array<T>) {
        this._list = initialValue || [];
    }
    public add(newItem: T) {
        const clone = this._list.map(i => this._deepCloneItem(i));
        const newList = [...clone, newItem];
        const newInstance = new ImmutableList<T>(newList);
        return newInstance;
    }
    public remove(
        item: T,
```

```typescript
        areEqual: (a: T, b: T) => boolean = (a, b) => a === b
    ) {
        const newList = this._list.filter(i => !areEqual(item, i))
                            .map(i => this._deepCloneItem(i));
        const newInstance = new ImmutableList<T>(newList);
        return newInstance;
    }
    public get(index: number): T | undefined {
        const item = this._list[index];
        return item ? this._deepCloneItem(item) : undefined;
    }
    public find(filter: (item: T) => boolean) {
        const item = this._list.find(filter);
        return item ? this._deepCloneItem(item) : undefined;
    }
}
```

Every time we add an item to, or remove it from, the immutable array, we create a new instance of the immutable array. This implementation is very inefficient, but it demonstrates the basic idea. We are going to create a quick test to demonstrate how the preceding class works. We are going to use some data regarding superheroes:

```typescript
interface Hero {
    name: string;
    powers: string[];
}

const heroes = [
    {
        name: "Spiderman",
        powers: [
            "wall-crawling",
            "enhanced strength",
            "enhanced speed",
            "spider-Sense"
        ]
    },
    {
        name: "Superman",
        powers: [
            "flight",
            "superhuman strength",
            "x-ray vision",
            "super-speed"
        ]
    }
];
```

```
const hulk = {
    name: "Hulk",
    powers: [
        "superhuman strength",
        "superhuman speed",
        "superhuman Stamina",
        "superhuman durability"
    ]
};
```

We can now use the preceding data to create a new immutable list instance. When we add a new superhero to the list, a new immutable list is created. If we try to search for the superhero Hulk in the two immutable lists, we will observe that only the second list contains it. We can also compare both lists to observe that they are two different objects, demonstrated as follows:

```
const myList = new ImmutableList<Hero>(heroes);
const myList2 = myList.add(hulk);
const result1 = myList.find((h => h.name === "Hulk"));
const result2 = myList2.find((h => h.name === "Hulk"));
const areEqual = myList2 === myList;

console.log(result1); // undefined
console.log(result2); // { name: "Hulk", powers: Array(4) }
console.log(areEqual); // false
```

Creating our own immutable data structures is, in most cases, not necessary. In a real-world application, we can use libraries such as Immutable.js to enjoy immutable data structures.

Functions as first-class citizens

It is common to find mentions of functions as **first-class citizens** in the FP literature. We say that a function is a first-class citizen when it can do everything that a variable can do, which means that functions can be passed to other functions as an argument. For example, the following function takes a function as its second argument:

```
function find<T>(arr: T[], filter: (i: T) => boolean) {
    return arr.filter(filter);
}

find(heroes, (h) => h.name === "Spiderman");
```

Or, it is returned by another function. For example, the following function takes a function as its only argument and returns a function:

```
function find<T>(filter: (i: T) => boolean) {
    return (arr: T[]) => {
        return arr.filter(filter);
    }
}
const findSpiderman = find((h: Hero) => h.name === "Spiderman");
const spiderman = findSpiderman(heroes);
```

Functions can also be assigned to variables. For example, in the preceding code snippet, we assigned the function returned by the find function to a variable named findSpiderman:

```
const findSpiderman = find((h: Hero) => h.name === "SPiderman");
```

Both JavaScript and TypeScript treat functions as first-class citizens.

Lambda expressions

Lambda expressions are just expressions that can be used to declare anonymous functions (functions without a name). Before the ES6 specification, the only way to assign a function as a value to a variable was to use a function expression:

```
const log = function(arg: any) { console.log(arg); };
```

The ES6 specification introduced the arrow function syntax:

```
const log = (arg: any) => console.log(arg);
```

 Please refer to Chapter 2, *Mastering Functions*, Chapter 4, *The Runtime – The Event Loop and the this Operator*, and Chapter 5, *The Runtime – Closures and Prototypes*, to learn more about arrow functions and function expressions.

Function arity

The **arity** of a function is the number of arguments that the function takes. A unary function is a function that only takes a single argument:

```
function isNull<T>(a: T|null) {
    return (a === null);
}
```

Unary functions are very important in functional programming because they facilitate utilization of the function composition pattern.

 We will learn more about function composition patterns later in Chapter 6, *Functional Programming Techniques*.

A binary function is a function that takes two arguments:

```
function add(a: number, b: number) {
    return a + b;
}
```

Functions with two or more arguments are also important because some of the most common FP patterns and techniques (for example, partial application and currying) have been designed to transform functions that allow multiple arguments into unary functions.

There are also functions with three (**ternary functions**) or more arguments. However, functions that accept a variable number of arguments, known as **variadic functions**, are particularly interesting in functional programming, as demonstrated in the following code snippet:

```
function addMany(...numbers: number[]) {
    numbers.reduce((p, c) => p + c, 0);
}
```

Higher-order functions

A higher-order function is a function that does at least one of the following:

- Takes one or more functions as arguments
- Returns a function as its result

Higher-order functions are some of the most powerful tools that we can use to write JavaScript in a functional programming style. Let's look at some examples.

The following code snippet declares a function named `addDelay`. The function creates a new function that waits for a given number of milliseconds before printing a message in the console. The function is considered a higher-order function because it returns a function:

```
function addDelay(msg: string, ms: number) {
    return () => {
        setTimeout(() => {
            console.log(msg);
        }, ms);
    };
}


const delayedSayHello = addDelay("Hello world!", 500);
delayedSayHello(); // Prints "Hello world!" (after 500 ms)
```

The following code snippet declares a function named `addDelay`. The function creates a new function that adds a delay in milliseconds to the execution of another function that is passed as an argument. The function is considered a higher-order function because it takes a function as an argument and returns a function:

```
function addDelay(func: () => void, ms: number) {
    return () => {
        setTimeout(() => {
            func();
        }, ms);
    };
}


function sayHello() {
    console.log("Hello world!");
}


const delayedSayHello = addDelay(sayHello, 500);
delayedSayHello(); // Prints "Hello world!" (after 500 ms)
```

Higher-order functions are an effective technique for abstracting a solution for a common problem. The preceding example demonstrates how we can use a higher-order function (`addDelay`) to add a delay to another function (`sayHello`). This technique allows us to abstract the delay functionality and keeps the `sayHello` function, or other functions, agnostic of the implementation details of the delay functionality.

Laziness

Many functional programming languages feature lazy-evaluated APIs. The idea behind lazy evaluation is that operations are not computed until doing so can no longer be postponed. The following example declares a function that allows us to find an element in an array. When the function is invoked, we don't filter the array. Instead, we declare a `proxy` and a `handler`:

```
function lazyFind<T>(arr: T[], filter: (i: T) => boolean): T {

    let hero: T | null = null;
    const proxy = new Proxy(
        {},
        {
            get: (obj, prop) => {
                console.log("Filtering...");
                if (!hero) {
                    hero = arr.find(filter) || null;
                }
                return hero ? (hero as any)[prop] : null;
            }
        }
    );

    return proxy as any;
}
```

It is only later, when one of the properties in the result is accessed, that the `proxy handler` is invoked and filtering takes place:

```
const heroes = [
    {
        name: "Spiderman",
        powers: [
            "wall-crawling",
            "enhanced strength",
            "enhanced speed",
            "spider-Sense"
        ]
    },
    {
        name: "Superman",
        powers: [
            "flight",
            "superhuman strength",
            "x-ray vision",
            "super-speed"
```

```
        ]
    }
];

console.log("A");
const spiderman = lazyFind(heroes, (h) => h.name === "Spiderman");
console.log("B");
console.log(spiderman.name);
console.log("C");

/*
    A
    B
    Filtering...
    Spiderman
    C
*/
```

If we examine the console output, we will be able to see that the **Filtering...** message is not logged into the console until we access the property name of the result object. The preceding implementation is a very rudimentary implementation, but it can help us to understand how lazy evaluation works. Laziness can sometimes improve the overall performance of our applications.

 We will learn more about function composition patterns later in Chapter 9, *Functional-Reactive Programming*.

Summary

In this chapter, we explored some of the most fundamental principles and concepts of the functional programming paradigm.

Over the next four chapters, we are going to deviate a little bit from functional programming because we are going to take an extensive look at functions, asynchronous programming, and certain aspects of the TypeScript/JavaScript runtime, such as closures and prototypes. We need to explore these topics before we can learn more about the implementation of functional programming techniques. However, if you are already very confident with using functions, closures, the this operator, and prototypes, then you should be able to skip the next four chapters.

2
Mastering Functions

In Chapter 1, *Functional Programming Fundamentals*, we learned about some of the most fundamental functional programming concepts. Functions are one of the fundamental building blocks of any TypeScript application, and they are powerful enough to warrant an entire chapter being dedicated to them in order to explore their potential.

In this chapter, we are going to master the usage of functions. The chapter starts with a quick recap of a number of basic concepts and then moves on to some less commonly known function features and use cases:

- **Function types**:
    - Function declarations and function expressions
    - Named and anonymous functions
- **Working with parameters**:
    - Functions with optional parameters
    - Functions with default parameters
    - Functions with rest parameters
    - Function overloading
    - Specialized overloading signature
- Function scope
- Immediately-invoked functions
- Tag functions and tagged templates

Function types

We already know that it is possible to explicitly declare the type of an element in our application by using optional type annotations:

```
function greetNamed(name: string): string {
    return 'Hi! ${name}';
}
```

In the previous function, we specified the type of parameter `name` (`string`) and its return type (`string`). Sometimes, we will need to specify the types of the function, as opposed to specifying the types of its components (arguments or returned value). Let's look at an example:

```
let greetUnnamed: (name: string) => string;

greetUnnamed = function(name: string): string {
    return 'Hi! ${name}';
};
```

In the preceding example, we have declared the `greetUnnamed` variable and its type. The `greetUnnamed` type is a function type that takes a string variable called `name` as its only parameter and returns a string after being invoked. After declaring the variable, a function, whose type must be equal to the variable type, is assigned to it.

We can also declare the `greetUnnamed` type and assign a function to it in the same line, rather than declaring it in two separate lines, as we did in the previous example:

```
let greetUnnamed: (name: string) => string = function(name: string): string
{
    return 'Hi! ${name}';
};
```

Just like in the previous example, the preceding code snippet also declares a variable, `greetUnnamed`, and its type. `greetUnnamed` is a function type that takes a string variable called `name` as its only parameter and will return a string after being invoked. We will assign a function to this variable in the same line in which it is declared. The type of the assigned function must match the variable type.

In the preceding example, we have declared the type of the greetUnnamed variable and then assigned a function as its value. The type of function can be inferred from the assigned function and, for this reason, it is unnecessary to add a redundant type annotation. We have done this to facilitate your understanding of this section, but it is important to mention that adding redundant type annotations can make our code harder to read, and is considered a bad practice.

Named and anonymous functions

Just as in JavaScript, TypeScript functions can be created either as a named function or as an anonymous function, which allows us to choose the most appropriate approach for an application, whether we are building a list of functions in an API or a one-off function to hand over to another function:

```
// named function
function greet(name?: string): string {
  if(name){
    return "Hi! " + name;
  } else {
    return "Hi!";
  }
}

// anonymous function
let greet = function(name?: string): string {
  if (name) {
    return "Hi! " + name;
  } else {
    return "Hi!";
  }
}
```

As we can see in the preceding code snippet, in TypeScript, we can add types to each of the parameters and then to the function itself to add a return type. TypeScript can infer the return type by looking at the return statements, so we can also optionally leave this off in many cases.

There is an alternative syntax for functions that use the `=>` operator after the `return` type and don't use the `function` keyword:

```
let greet = (name: string): string => {
    if(name){
      return "Hi! " + name;
    }
    else
    {
      return "Hi";
    }
};
```

Now that we have learned about this alternative syntax, we can return to the previous example in which we were assigning an anonymous function to the `greet` variable. We can now add type annotations to the `greet` variable to match the `anonymous` function signature:

```
let greet: (name: string) => string = function(name: string):
string {
    if (name) {
      return "Hi! " + name;
    } else {
      return "Hi!";
    }
};
```

 Keep in mind that the arrow function (=>) syntax changes the way the `this` operator works when working with classes. We will learn more about this in upcoming chapters.

The previous code snippet demonstrates how to use type annotations to force a variable to be a function with a specific signature. These kinds of annotation are commonly used when we annotate a `callback` (a function used as an argument of another function):

```
function add(
    a: number,
    b: number,
    callback: (result: number) => void
) {
    callback(a + b);
}
```

In the preceding example, we are declaring a function named `add` that takes two numbers and a `callback` as a function. The type annotations will force the `callback` to return `void` and take a number as its only argument.

Function declarations and function expressions

In the preceding section, we introduced the possibility of declaring functions with (a named function) or without (an unnamed or anonymous function) explicitly indicating their name, but we didn't mention that we were also using two different types of function.

In the following example, the named function, `greetNamed`, is a **function declaration** while `greetUnnamed` is a **function expression**. For the time being, please ignore the first two lines, which contain two `console.log` statements:

```
console.log(greetNamed("John")); // OK
console.log(greetUnnamed("John")); // Error

function greetNamed(name: string): string {
    return 'Hi! ${name}';
}

let greetUnnamed = function(name: string): string {
    return 'Hi! ${name}';
};
```

We might think that the preceding functions are identical, but they behave differently. The JavaScript interpreter can evaluate a function declaration as it is being parsed. On the other hand, the `function` expression is part of an assignment and will not be evaluated until the assignment has been completed.

> The primary cause of the different behavior of these functions is a process known as variable **hoisting**. We will learn more about the variable hoisting process in the *Function scope and hoisting* section later in this chapter.

Fortunately, the TypeScript compiler can detect this error and throw a compilation-time error. However, if we compile the preceding TypeScript code snippet into JavaScript, ignore the compilation errors, and try to execute it in a web browser, we will observe that the first `console.log` call works. This is the case because JavaScript knows about the declaration function and can parse it before the program is executed.

However, the second alert statement will throw an exception, to indicate that greetUnnamed is not a function. The exception is thrown because the greetUnnamed assignment must be completed before the function can be evaluated.

Working with function parameters

In this section, we are going to learn how to work with function parameters in multiple scenarios, including optional parameters, default parameters, and rest parameters.

Trailing commas in function arguments

Trailing commas are commas that are used after the final argument of a function. Using a comma after the last parameter of a function can be useful because it is very common to forget a comma when we modify an existing function by adding additional parameters.

For example, the following function only takes one parameter and doesn't use trailing commas:

```
function greetWithoutTralingCommas(
    name: string
): string {
    return 'Hi! ${name}';
}
```

Some time after the initial implementation, we might be required to add a parameter to the previous function. A common mistake is to declare the new parameter and forget to add a comma after the first parameter:

```
function updatedGreetWithoutTralingCommas(
    name: string
    surname: string, // Error
): string {
    return 'Hi! ${name} ${surname}';
}
```

Using a trailing comma in the first version of the function could have helped us to prevent this common mistake:

```
function greetWithTralingCommas(
    name: string,
): string {
    return 'Hi! ${name}';
}
```

Using a trailing comma eliminates the possibility of forgetting the comma when adding a new argument:

```
function updatedGreetWithTralingCommas(
    name: string,
    surname: string,
): string {
    return 'Hi! ${name} ${surname}';
}
```

 TypeScript will throw an error if we forget a comma, so trailing commas are not needed as much as they are when working with JavaScript. Trailing commas are optional, but using them is considered good practice by many JavaScript and TypeScript engineers.

Functions with optional parameters

Unlike JavaScript, the TypeScript compiler will throw an error if we attempt to invoke a function without providing the exact number and types of parameters that its signature declares. Let's look at a code sample to demonstrate it:

```
function add(foo: number, bar: number, foobar: number): number {
    return foo + bar + foobar;
}
```

The preceding function is called `add` and will take three numbers as parameters, named `foo`, `bar`, and `foobar`. If we attempt to invoke this function without providing exactly three numbers, we will get a compilation error indicating that the supplied parameters do not match the function's signature:

```
add(); // Error, expected 3 arguments, but got 0.
add(2, 2); // Error, expected 3 arguments, but got 2.
add(2, 2, 2); // OK, returns 6
```

There are scenarios in which we might want to be able to call the function without providing all of its arguments. TypeScript features optional parameters in functions to help us to increase the flexibility of our functions and overcome such scenarios.

We can indicate to the TypeScript compiler that we want a function's parameter to be optional by appending the character ? to its name. Let's update the previous function to transform the required parameter, `foobar`, into an optional parameter:

```
function add(foo: number, bar: number, foobar?: number): number {
    let result = foo + bar;
```

```
    if (foobar !== undefined) {
        result += foobar;
    }
    return result;
}
```

Note how we have changed the `foobar` parameter name into `foobar?` and are checking the `foobar` type inside the function to identify whether the parameter was supplied as an argument to the function. After implementing these changes, the TypeScript compiler will allow us to invoke the function without errors when we supply two or three arguments to it:

```
add(); // Error, expected 2-3 arguments, but got 0.
add(2, 2); // OK, returns 4
add(2, 2, 2); // OK, returns 6
```

It is important to note that the optional parameters must always be located after the requisite parameters in the function's parameter list.

Functions with default parameters

When a function has some optional parameters, we must check whether an argument has been passed to the function (just like we did in the previous example) to prevent potential errors.

There are a number of scenarios in which it would be more useful to provide a default value for a parameter when it is not supplied than to make it an optional parameter. Let's rewrite the `add` function (from the previous section) using the inline `if` structure:

```
function add(foo: number, bar: number, foobar?: number): number {
    return foo + bar + (foobar !== undefined ? foobar : 0);
}
```

There is nothing wrong with the preceding function, but we can improve its readability by providing a default value for the `foobar` parameter instead of using an `optional` parameter:

```
function add(foo: number, bar: number, foobar: number = 0): number {
    return foo + bar + foobar;
}
```

To indicate that a `function` parameter is optional, we need to provide a default value using the = operator when declaring the function's signature. After compiling the preceding examples, the TypeScript compiler will generate an `if` statement in the JavaScript output to set a default value for the `foobar` parameter if it is not passed as an argument to the `function`:

```
function add(foo, bar, foobar) {
    if (foobar === void 0) { foobar = 0; }
    return foo + bar + foobar;
}
```

This is great because the TypeScript compiler generated the code required to prevent potential runtime errors for us.

The `void 0` parameter is used by the TypeScript compiler to check whether a variable is equal to undefined. While most developers use the `undefined` variable to perform this kind of check, most compilers use `void 0` because it will always evaluate as undefined. Checking against `undefined` is less secure because its value could have been modified, as demonstrated by the following code snippet:

```
function test() {
    var undefined = 2; // 2
    console.log(undefined === 2); // true
}
```

Just like `optional` parameters, `default` parameters must always be located after any required parameters in the function's parameter list.

Functions with rest parameters

We have learned how to use `optional` and `default` parameters to increase the number of ways that we can invoke a function. Let's return to the previous example one more time:

```
function add(foo: number, bar: number, foobar: number = 0): number {
    return foo + bar + foobar;
}
```

We have learned how to invoke the `add` function with two or three parameters, but what if we wanted to allow other developers to pass four or five parameters to our function? We would have to add two extra `default` or `optional` parameters. And what if we wanted to allow them to pass as many parameters as they need? The solution to this possible scenario is the use of `rest` parameters. The `rest` parameter syntax allows us to represent an indefinite number of arguments as an array:

```
function add(...foo: number[]): number {
    let result = 0;
    for (let i = 0; i < foo.length; i++) {
        result += foo[i];
    }
    return result;

}
```

As we can see in the preceding code snippet, we have replaced the `function` parameters `foo`, `bar`, and `foobar`, with just one parameter named `foo`. Note that the name of the parameter `foo` is preceded by an ellipsis (a set of three periods—not the actual ellipsis character). A `rest` parameter must be of an array type, or we will get a compilation error. We can now invoke the `add` function with as many parameters as we need:

```
add(); // 0
add(2); // 2
add(2, 2); // 4
add(2, 2, 2); // 6
add(2, 2, 2, 2); // 8
add(2, 2, 2, 2, 2); // 10
add(2, 2, 2, 2, 2, 2); // 12
```

Although there is no specific limit in the theoretical maximum number of arguments that a function can take, there are, of course, practical limits. These limits are entirely implementation-dependent and, most likely, will also depend exactly on how we are calling the function.

JavaScript functions have a built-in object called the `arguments` object. This object is available as a local variable named arguments. The `arguments` variable contains an object such as an array, which includes the arguments used when the function was invoked.

> The `arguments` object exposes some of the methods and properties provided by a standard array, but not all of them. Refer to the complete reference at `https://developer.mozilla.org/en-US/docs/Web/JavaScript/Reference/Functions/arguments` to learn more about its peculiarities.

If we examine the JavaScript output, we will notice that TypeScript iterates the `arguments` object to add the values to the `foo` variable:

```
function add() {
    var foo = [];
    for (var _i = 0; _i < arguments.length; _i++) {
        foo[_i - 0] = arguments[_i];
    }
    var result = 0;
    for (var i = 0; i < foo.length; i++) {
        result += foo[i];
    }
    return result;
}
```

We can argue that this is an extra, unnecessary iteration over the function's parameters. Even though it is hard to imagine this further iteration becoming a performance issue, if you think that this could be a problem in terms of the performance of your application, you may want to consider avoiding the use of `rest` parameters and use an array as the only parameter of the function instead:

```
function add(foo: number[]): number {
    let result = 0;
    for (let i = 0; i < foo.length; i++) {
        result += foo[i];
    }
    return result;
}
```

The preceding function takes an array of numbers as its only parameter. The invocation API will be a little bit different from the `rest` parameters, but we will effectively avoid the extra iteration over the function's argument list:

```
add(); // Error, expected 1 argument, but got 0.
add(2); // Error, '2' is not assignable to parameter of type 'number[]'.
add(2, 2); // Error, expected 1 argument, but got 2.
add(2, 2, 2); // Error, expected 1 argument, but got 3.
add([]); // returns 0
add([2]); // returns 2
add([2, 2]); // returns 4
add([2, 2, 2]); // returns 6
```

The following table summarizes the parameter-related features that we have explored in this section:

Name	Operator	Description
Trailing commas	,	Used to facilitate adding additional parameters to an existing function at a later time.
Optional parameters	?	Used to describe optional arguments. When the argument is missed, the value of the parameter is undefined.
Default parameters	=	Used to describe optional arguments. When the argument is missed, the value of the parameter takes a default value.
Rest parameters	. . .	Used to describe functions with an unknown number of arguments.

In the following section, we are going to learn about function overloading.

Function overloading

Function, or method, overloading is the ability to create multiple methods with the same name and a different number of parameters or types. In TypeScript, we can overload a function by specifying all function signatures (known as **overload signatures**) of a function, followed by a signature (known as the **implementation signature**). Let's look at an example:

```typescript
function test(name: string): string; // overloaded signature
function test(age: number): string; // overloaded signature
function test(single: boolean): string; // overloaded signature
function test(value: (string|number|boolean)): string { // implementation
signature
    switch (typeof value) {
        case "string":
            return 'My name is ${value}.';
        case "number":
            return 'I'm ${value} years old.';
        case "boolean":
            return value ? "I'm single." : "I'm not single.";
        default:
            throw new Error("Invalid Operation!");
    }
}
```

As we can see in the preceding example, we have overloaded the function test three times by adding a signature that takes a string as its only parameter, another function that takes a number, and a final signature that takes a Boolean as its unique parameter. It is important to note that all function signatures must be compatible; so, if, for example, one of the signatures tries to return a number while another tries to return a string, we will get a compilation error:

```
function test(name: string): string;
function test(age: number): number; // Error
function test(single: boolean): string;
function test(value: (string|number|boolean)): string {
    switch (typeof value) {
        case "string":
            return 'My name is ${value}.';
        case "number":
            return 'I'm ${value} years old.';
        case "boolean":
            return value ? "I'm single." : "I'm not single.";
        default:
            throw new Error("Invalid Operation!");
    }
}
```

 Please note that this restriction can be overcome by using a specialized overloaded signature, as we will learn in the following section.

The implementation signature must be compatible with all the overloaded signatures, always be the last in the list, and take any or a union type as the type of its parameters.

Invoking the function by providing arguments that don't match any of the types declared by the overload signatures will lead to a compilation error:

```
test("Remo"); // returns "My name is Remo."
test(29); // returns "I'm 29 years old.";
test(false); // returns "I'm not single.";
test({ custom: "custom" }); // Error
```

Specialized overloading signature

We can use a specialized signature to create multiple methods with the same name and number of parameters, but a different return type. To create a specialized signature, we must indicate the type of function parameter using a string. The string literal is used to identify which of the function overloads is invoked:

```
interface Document {
    createElement(tagName: "div"): HTMLDivElement; // specialized
    createElement(tagName: "span"): HTMLSpanElement; // specialized
    createElement(tagName: "canvas"): HTMLCanvasElement; // specialized
    createElement(tagName: string): HTMLElement; // non-specialized
}
```

In the preceding example, we have declared three **specialized overloaded signatures** and one **non-specialized signature** for the function named `createElement`.

When we declare a specialized signature in an object, it must be assignable to at least one non-specialized signature in the same object. This can be observed in the preceding example, as the `createElement` property belongs to a type that contains three specialized signatures, all of which are assignable to the non-specialized signature in the type.

When writing overloaded declarations, we must list the non-specialized signature last.

Function scope and hoisting

Low-level languages, such as C, have low-level memory management features. In programming languages with a higher level of abstraction, such as TypeScript, values are allocated when variables are created, and automatically cleared from memory when they are no longer used. The process that cleans the memory is known as **garbage collection** and is performed by the JavaScript runtime garbage collector.

The garbage collector does a great job, but it is a mistake to assume that it will always prevent us from facing a memory leak. The garbage collector will clear a variable from the memory whenever the variable is out of scope. It is important to understand how the TypeScript scope works in order for us to understand the life cycle of variables.

Some programming languages use the structure of the program source code to determine what variables we are referring to (**lexical scoping**), while others use the runtime state of the program stack to determine what variable we are referring to (**dynamic scoping**). Most modern programming languages use lexical scoping (including TypeScript). Lexical scoping tends to be dramatically easier to understand for both humans and analysis tools than dynamic scoping.

While, in most lexical-scoped programming languages, variables are scoped to a block (a section of code delimited by curly braces { }), in TypeScript (and JavaScript) variables are scoped to a function, as demonstrated by the following code snippet:

```
function foo(): void {
    if (true) {
        var bar: number = 0;
    }
    console.log(bar);
}

foo(); // 0
```

The preceding function, named `foo`, contains an `if` structure. We have declared a numeric variable named `bar` inside the `if` statement, and later we have attempted to show the value of the `bar` variable using the `log` function.

We might think that the preceding code sample would throw an error in the fifth line because the `bar` variable should be out of scope when the `log` function is invoked. However, if we invoke the `foo` function, the `log` function will be able to display the variable `bar` without errors because all variables inside a function will be within the scope of the entire function body, even if they are inside another block of code (except a function block).

The following diagram displays the lexical scope at the function level (left), and the lexical scope at the block level (right). As we can see, there is only one function, but there are two blocks:

```typescript
function foo(): void {            function foo(): void {
    if (true) {                       if (true) {
        var bar: number = 0;              var bar: number = 0;
    }                                 }
    console.log(bar);                 console.log(bar);
}                                 }

foo(); // 0                       foo(); // 0
```

The preceding code snippet might seem confusing, but it is easy to understand once we know that, at runtime, all the variable declarations are moved to the top of a function before the function is executed. This behavior is known as **hoisting**.

 TypeScript is compiled to JavaScript and then executed—this means that a TypeScript application is a JavaScript application at runtime and, for this reason, when we refer to the TypeScript runtime, we are talking about the JavaScript runtime. We will learn in depth about the runtime in Chapter 4, *The Runtime – The Event Loop and The this Operator*, and Chapter 5, *The Runtime – Closures and Prototypes*.

Before the preceding code snippet is executed, the runtime will move the declaration of the bar variable to the top of our function:

```typescript
function foo() {
    var bar;
    if (true) {
        bar = 0;
    }
    console.log(bar);
}

foo(); // 0
```

This explains why it is possible to use a variable before it is declared. Let's look at an example:

```
function foo (): void {
    bar = 0;
    var bar: number;
    console.log(bar);
}

foo(); // 0
```

In the preceding code snippet, we have declared a function, foo, and, in its body, we have assigned the value 0 to a variable named bar. At this point, the variable has not been declared. In the second line, we are declaring the bar variable and its type. In the last line, we are displaying the value of the bar variable using the alert function.

Since declaring a variable anywhere inside a function (except another function) is equivalent to declaring it at the top of the function, the foo function is transformed into the following at runtime:

```
function foo (): void {
    var bar: number;
    bar = 0;
    console.log(bar);
}

foo(); // 0
```

Developers with a background in programming languages with block scope, such as Java or C#, are not used to function scope and it is one of the most criticized characteristics of JavaScript. The people in charge of the development of the ECMAScript 6 specification are aware of this, and, as a result, they have introduced the keywords let and const.

The let keyword allows us to set the scope of a variable to a block (if, while, for, and so on) rather than a function. We can update the first example in this section to showcase how the let keyword works:

```
function foo (): void {
    if (true) {
        let bar: number = 0;
        bar = 1;
    }
    console.log(bar); // Error
}
```

The `bar` variable is now declared using the `let` keyword, and, as a result, it is only accessible inside the `if` block. The variable is not hoisted to the top of the `foo` function and cannot be accessed by the `alert` function outside the `if` statement.

While variables defined with `const` follow the same scope rules as variables declared with `let`, they can't be reassigned:

```
function foo(): void {
    if (true) {
        const bar: number = 0;
        bar = 1; // Error
    }
    alert(bar); // Error
}
```

If we attempt to compile the preceding code snippet, we will get an error because the `bar` variable is not accessible outside the `if` statement (just like when we used the `let` keyword), and a new error occurs when we try to assign a new value to the `bar` variable. The second error is caused because it is not possible to assign a new value to a constant variable once the variable has already been initialized.

 Variables declared with the `const` keyword cannot be reassigned, but are not immutable. When we say that a variable is immutable, we mean that it cannot be modified. We will learn more about immutability in `Chapter 9`, *Functional-Reactive Programming*.

Immediately-invoked functions

An **immediately-invoked function expression (IIFE)** is a design pattern that produces a lexical scope using function scoping. IIFE can be used to avoid variable hoisting from within blocks or to prevent us from polluting the global scope, for example:

```
let bar = 0; // global

(function() {
    let foo: number = 0; // In scope of this function
    bar = 1; // Access global scope
    console.log(bar); // 1
    console.log(foo); // 0
})();

console.log(bar); // 1
console.log(foo); // Error
```

In the preceding example, we have wrapped the declaration of a variable (foo) with an IIFE. The foo variable is scoped to the IIFE function and is not available in the global scope, which explains the error when trying to access it on the last line.

The bar variable is global. Therefore, it can be accessed from within and from outside the IIFE function.

We can also pass a variable to the IIFE to have better control over the creation of variables outside its scope:

```
let bar = 0; // global
let topScope = window;

(function(global: any) {
    let foo: number = 0; // In scope of this function
    console.log(global.bar); // 0
    global.bar = 1; // Access global scope
    console.log(global.bar); // 1
    console.log(foo); // 0
}) (topScope);

console.log(bar); // 1
console.log(foo); // Error
```

Furthermore, IIFE can help us to simultaneously allow public access to methods while retaining privacy for variables defined within the function. Let's look at an example:

```
class Counter {
    private _i: number;
    public constructor() {
        this._i = 0;
    }
    public get(): number {
        return this._i;
    }
    public set(val: number): void {
        this._i = val;
    }
    public increment(): void {
        this._i++;
    }
}

let counter = new Counter();
console.log(counter.get()); // 0
counter.set(2);
console.log(counter.get()); // 2
```

```
counter.increment();
console.log(counter.get()); // 3
console.log(counter._i); // Error: Property '_i' is private
```

We have defined a class named `Counter`, which has a private numerical attribute named `_i`. The class also has methods to get and set the value of the `_i` private property.

 By convention, TypeScript and JavaScript developers usually name private variables with names preceded by the underscore character (_).

We have also created an instance of the `Counter` class and invoked the methods `set`, `get`, and `increment` to observe that everything is working as expected. If we attempt to access the `_i` property in an instance of `Counter`, we will get an error because the variable is private.

If we compile the preceding TypeScript code (only the class definition) and examine the JavaScript code generated, we will see the following:

```
var Counter = (function() {
    function Counter() {
        this._i = 0;
    }

    Counter.prototype.get = function() {
        return this._i;
    };

    Counter.prototype.set = function(val) {
        this._i = val;
    };

    Counter.prototype.increment = function() {
        this._i++;
    };

    return Counter;
})();
```

This generated JavaScript code will work perfectly in most scenarios, but if we execute it in a browser and try to create an instance of `Counter` and access its property `_i`, we will not get any errors because TypeScript will not generate runtime private properties for us. Occasionally, we will need to write our classes in such a way that some properties are private at runtime, for example, if we release a library that will be used by JavaScript developers.

We can also use IIFE to simultaneously allow public access to methods while retaining privacy for variables defined within the function:

```
var Counter = (function() {
    var _i: number = 0;
    function Counter() {
        //
    }
    Counter.prototype.get = function() {
        return _i;
    };
    Counter.prototype.set = function(val: number) {
        _i = val;
    };
    Counter.prototype.increment = function() {
        _i++;
    };
    return Counter;
})();
```

In the preceding example, everything is almost identical to TypeScript's generated JavaScript, except that the variable _i is now an object in the Counter closure instead of a property of the Counter class.

> Closures are functions that refer to independent (free) variables. In other words, the function defined in the closure remembers the environment (variables in the scope) in which it was created. We will discover more about closures in Chapter 5, *The Runtime – Closures and Prototypes*.

If we run the generated JavaScript output in a browser and try to invoke the _i property directly, we will notice that the property is now private at runtime:

```
let counter = new Counter();
console.log(counter.get()); // 0
counter.set(2);
console.log(counter.get()); // 2
counter.increment();
console.log(counter.get()); // 3
console.log(counter._i); // undefined
```

In some cases, we will need to have precise control over scope and closures, and our code will end up looking much more like JavaScript. If we write our application components (classes, modules, and so on) to be consumed by other TypeScript components, we will rarely have to worry about implementing runtime private properties. We will look in depth at the TypeScript runtime in Chapter 4, *The Runtime – The Event Loop and The this Operator,* and Chapter 5, *The Runtime – Closures and Prototypes.*

Tag functions and tagged templates

In TypeScript, we can use template strings such as the following:

```
let name = "remo";
let surname = "jansen";
let html = '<h1>${name} ${surname}</h1>';
```

We can use a template string to create a special kind of function known as a **tag function**.

We can use a tag function to extend or modify the standard behavior of template strings. When we apply a tag function to a template string, the template string becomes a tagged template.

We are going to implement a tag function named htmlEscape. To use a tag function, we must use the name of the function, followed by a template string:

```
let html = htmlEscape '<h1>${name} ${surname}</h1>';
```

A tag template must return a string and take the following arguments:

- A TemplateStringsArray, which contains all the static literals in the template string (<h1> and </h1> in the preceding example), is passed as the first argument.

The TemplateStringsArray type is declared by the lib.d.ts file. The lib.d.ts file contains the type declarations of the native JavaScript and browser APIs.

- A rest parameter is passed as the second parameter. The rest parameter contains all the values in the template string (name and surname in the preceding example).

The signature of a `tag` function appears as follows:

```
tag(literals: TemplateStringsArray, ...placeholders: any[]): string;
```

Let's implement the `htmlEscape` tag function:

```
function htmlEscape(literals: TemplateStringsArray, ...placeholders: any[])
{
    let result = "";
    for (let i = 0; i < placeholders.length; i++) {
        result += literals[i];
        result += placeholders[i]
            .replace(/&/g, "&amp;")
            .replace(/"/g, "&quot;")
            .replace(/"/g, "'")
            .replace(/</g, "&lt;")
            .replace(/>/g, "&gt;");
    }
    result += literals[literals.length - 1];
    return result;
}
```

We can then invoke the function as follows:

```
let html = htmlEscape '<h1>${name} ${surname}</h1>';
```

The template string contains values and literals. The `htmlEscape` function iterates through them and ensures that the HTML code is escaped in the values to avoid possible code injection attacks.

The main benefit of using a tagged function is that it allows us to create custom template string processors.

Summary

In this chapter, we have learned a lot about functions. We have learned about different kinds of functions, such as named and anonymous function, and function declarations and function expressions. We also learned how to declare different types of function signatures as well as how to work with function arguments in multiple scenarios.

In the next chapter, we are going to learn about asynchronous programming techniques. We will learn why functions play a very fundamental role in the TypeScript and JavaScript asynchronous programming model.

3
Mastering Asynchronous Programming

In the previous chapter, we learned how to work with functions. In this chapter, we will explore how we can use functions, together with some native APIs, to write asynchronous TypeScript code. We will focus on TypeScript's asynchronous programming capabilities, including the following concepts:

- Callbacks and higher-order functions
- Arrow functions
- Callback hell
- Promises
- Generators
- Asynchronous functions (`async` and `await`)

Callbacks and higher-order functions

In TypeScript, functions can be passed as arguments to another function. Functions can also be returned by another function. A function passed to another as an argument is known as a **callback**. A function that accepts functions as parameters (callbacks) or returns functions is known as a **higher-order function**.

Callback are usually anonymous functions. They can be declared before they are passed to the higher-order function, as demonstrated by the following example:

```
var myCallback = function() { // callback
  console.log("foo");
}

function bar(cb: () => void) { // higher order function
  console.log("bar");
```

```
    cb();
}

bar(myCallback); // prints "bar" then prints "foo"
```

Callbacks can also be declared inline, at the same point in which they are passed to a higher-order function, as demonstrated by the following example:

```
bar(() => {
    console.log("foo");
}); // prints "bar" then prints "foo"
```

The preceding code snippet declares an anonymous function and passes it to a function named `bar`. The anonymous function has been declared using an alternative syntax known as an arrow function. We will learn more about arrow functions in the next section.

Arrow functions

In TypeScript, we can declare a function using a function expression or an arrow function. An arrow function expression has a shorter syntax than a function expression and lexically binds the value of the `this` operator.

The `this` operator behaves a little differently in TypeScript and JavaScript compared to other popular programming languages. When we define a class in TypeScript, we can use the `this` operator to refer to the class. Let's look at an example:

```
class Person {
    private _name: string;
    constructor(name: string) {
        this._name = name;
    }
    public greet() {
        console.log('Hi! My name is ${this._name}');
    }
}

let person = new Person("Remo");
person.greet(); // "Hi! My name is Remo"
```

We have defined a class named `Person` that contains a property of the `string` type called name. The class has a constructor and a method named `greet`. We have created an instance named `person` and invoked the `greet` method, which internally uses the `this` operator to access the _name property. Inside the `greet` method, the `this` operator points to the object that encloses the `greet` method (the class instance).

We must be careful when using the `this` operator because, in some scenarios, it can point to the wrong value. Let's add an extra method to the previous example:

```
class Person {
    private _name: string;
    constructor(name: string) {
        this._name = name;
    }

    public greet() {
        alert('Hi! My name is ${this._name}');
    }

    public greetDelay(time: number) {
        setTimeout(function() {
            alert('Hi! My name is ${this._name}'); // Error
        }, time);
    }

}

let person = new Person("Remo");
person.greetDelay(1000); // Error
```

In the `greetDelay` method, we perform an almost identical operation to the one performed by the `greet` method. This time, the function takes a parameter named `time`, which is used to delay the `greet` message.

To delay a message, we use the `setTimeout` function and a callback. As soon as we define an anonymous function (the callback), the `this` keyword changes its value and starts pointing to the anonymous function, which explains why the TypeScript compiler will throw an error.

As mentioned, an arrow function expression lexically binds the value of the `this` operator. This means that it allows us to add a function without altering the value of this operator. Let's replace the function expression from the previous example with an arrow function:

```
class Person {

    private _name: string;

    constructor(name: string) {
        this._name = name;
    }

    public greet() {
```

```
            alert('Hi! My name is ${this._name}');
    }

    public greetDelay(time: number) {
        setTimeout(() => {
            alert('Hi! My name is ${this._name}'); // OK
        }, time);
    }

}

let person = new Person("Remo");
person.greet(); // "Hi! My name is Remo"
person.greetDelay(1000); // "Hi! My name is Remo"
```

By using an arrow function, we can ensure that the this operator still points to the Person instance and not to the setTimeout callback. If we execute the greetDelay function, the name property will be displayed as expected.

The following piece of code is generated by the TypeScript compiler. When compiling an arrow function, the TypeScript compiler will generate an alias for the this operator named _this. The alias is used to ensure that the this operator points to the correct object:

```
Person.prototype.greetDelay = function (time) {
    var _this = this;
    setTimeout(function () {
        alert("Hi! My name is " + _this._name);
    }, time);
};
```

 We will look in depth at the this operator in Chapter 4, *The Runtime – The Event Loop and* the this *Operator*.

Callback hell

We have learned that callbacks and higher-order functions are two powerful and flexible JavaScript and TypeScript features. However, the use of callbacks can lead to a maintainability issue known as callback hell.

We are now going to write an example to showcase callback hell. We are going to write three functions with the same behavior.

The first function is named `doSomethingAsync`. The function takes an array of numbers as one of its arguments and adds a new number to it. The function uses `setTimeout` to simulate some I/O operation, such as reading from a database, and `Math.ramdom` to simulate a potential exception, such as a request timeout:

```
function doSomethingAsync(
    arr: number[],
    success: (arr: number[]) => void,
    error: (e: Error) => void
) {
    setTimeout(() => {
        try {
            let n = Math.ceil(Math.random() * 100 + 1);
            if (n < 25) {
                throw new Error("n is < 25");
            }
            success([...arr, n]);
        } catch (e) {
            error(e);
        }
    }, 1000);
}
```

The second function is named `doSomethingElseAsync`, and the third and final function is named `doSomethingMoreAsync`. We are going to skip the implementation of these two functions in the following code snippet because both functions have the exact same implementation that we used in the `doSomethingAsync` function:

```
function doSomethingElseAsync(
    arr: number[],
    success: (arr: number[]) => void,
    error: (e: Error) => void
) {
    // ... Same implementation here...
}

function doSomethingMoreAsync(
    arr: number[],
    success: (arr: number[]) => void,
    error: (e: Error) => void
) {
    // Same imlementation here...
}
```

The preceding functions simulate an asynchronous operation by using the `setTimeout` function. Each function takes a `success` callback, which is invoked if the operation is successful, and an `error` callback, which is invoked if something goes wrong.

In real-world applications, asynchronous operations usually involve some interaction with hardware (for example, the filesystem, network...). These interactions are known as **input/output (I/O)** operations. I/O operations can fail for many different reasons; for example, we get an error when we try to interact with the filesystem to save a new file and there is not enough space available in the hard disk.

The preceding functions generate a random number and throw an error if the number is lower than 25; we do this to simulate potential I/O errors. They then add the random number to an array that is passed as an argument to each of the functions. If no errors take place, the result of the final function (`doSomethingMoreAsync`) should be an array with three random numbers.

Now that the three functions have been declared, we can try to invoke them in order. We are going to use callbacks to ensure that `doSomethingMoreAsync` is invoked after `doSomethingElseAsync`, and that `doSomethingElseAsync` is invoked after `doSomethingAsync`:

```
doSomethingAsync([], (arr1) => {
    doSomethingElseAsync(arr1, (arr2) => {
        doSomethingMoreAsync(arr2, (arr3) => {
            console.log(
                `
                doSomethingAsync: ${arr3[0]}
                doSomethingElseAsync: ${arr3[1]}
                doSomethingMoreAsync: ${arr3[2]}
                `
            );
        }, (e) => console.log(e));
    }, (e) => console.log(e));
}, (e) => console.log(e));
```

The preceding example used a few nesting callbacks. These kinds of nested callbacks are known as callback hell because they can lead to some maintainability issues, as follows:

- They make the code harder to follow and understand
- They make the code harder to maintain (refactor, reuse, and so on)
- They make exception handling more difficult

Promises

After seeing how the use of callbacks can lead to some maintainability problems, we are now going to learn about promises and how they can be used to write better asynchronous code. The core idea behind promises is that a promise represents the result of an asynchronous operation. A promise must be in one of the following three states:

- **Pending**: The initial state of a promise.
- **Fulfilled**: Also known as resolved, this the state of a promise representing a successful operation. The terms *fulfilled* and *resolved* are both commonly used to refer to this state.
- **Rejected**: The state of a promise representing a failed operation.

Once a promise is fulfilled or rejected, its state can never change again. Let's look at the basic syntax of a promise:

```
function foo() {
    return new Promise<string>((fulfill, reject) => {
        try {
            // do something
            fulfill("SomeValue");
        } catch (e) {
            reject(e);
        }
    });
}

foo().then((value) => {
    console.log(value);
}).catch((e) => {
    console.log(e);
});
```

 Please note that a try...catch statement is used here to showcase how we can explicitly fulfill or reject a promise. The try...catch statement is not needed for a Promise function because, when an error is thrown within a promise, the promise will automatically be rejected.

The preceding code snippet declares a function named foo that returns a promise. The promise contains a method named then, which accepts a callback function as an argument. The callback function is invoked when the promise is fulfilled. Promises also provide a method named catch, which is invoked when a promise is rejected.

Promises will not be recognized by the TypeScript compiler if we are targeting ES5 because the `Promise` API is part of ES6. We can solve this by enabling the `es2015.promise` type using the `lib` option in the `tsconfig.json` file. Note that enabling this option will disable some types that are included by default and thereby break some examples. You will be able to resolve the problems by including the `dom` and `es5` types as well by using the lib option in the `tsconfig.json` file:

```
"lib": [
    "es2015.promise",
    "dom",
    "es5",
    "es2015.generator", // new
    "es2015.iterable" // new
]
```

We are now going to rewrite the `doSomethingAsync`, `doSomethingElseAsync`, and `doSomethingMoreAsync` functions, which we wrote in the *Callback hell* section, but this time, we are going to use promises instead of callbacks:

```
function doSomethingAsync(arr: number[]) {
    return new Promise<number[]>((resolve, reject) => {
        setTimeout(() => {
            try {
                let n = Math.ceil(Math.random() * 100 + 1);
                if (n < 25) {
                    throw new Error("n is < 25");
                }
                resolve([...arr, n]);
            } catch (e) {
                reject(e);
            }
        }, 1000);
    });
}
```

Once again, we are going to skip the implementation details of the `doSomethingElseAsync` and `doSomethingMoreAsync` functions because they should be identical to the implementation of the `doSomethingAsync` function:

```
function doSomethingElseAsync(arr: number[]) {
    // Same implementation here...
}
```

```
function doSomethingMoreAsync(arr: number[]) {
    // Same implementation here...
}
```

We can chain the promises returned by each of the preceding functions using the Promise API:

```
doSomethingAsync([]).then((arr1) => {
    doSomethingElseAsync(arr1).then((arr2) => {
        doSomethingMoreAsync(arr2).then((arr3) => {
            console.log(
                `
                doSomethingAsync: ${arr3[0]}
                doSomethingElseAsync: ${arr3[1]}
                doSomethingMoreAsync: ${arr3[2]}
                `
            );
        });
    });
}).catch((e) => console.log(e));
```

The preceding code snippet is a little better than the one used in the callback example, because we only needed to declare one instead of three exception handlers. This is possible because errors are propagated through the chain of promises. However, we can improve the code even more because the Promise API allows us to chain promises in a much less verbose manner:

```
doSomethingAsync([])
    .then(doSomethingElseAsync)
    .then(doSomethingMoreAsync)
    .then((arr3) => {
        console.log(
            `
            doSomethingAsync: ${arr3[0]}
            doSomethingElseAsync: ${arr3[1]}
            doSomethingMoreAsync: ${arr3[2]}
            `
        );
    }).catch((e) => console.log(e));
```

The preceding code is much easier to read and follow than the one used during the callback examples, but this is not the only reason to favor promises over callbacks. Using promises also gives us better control over the execution flow of operations. Let's look at a couple of examples.

The `Promise` API includes a method named `all`, which allows us to execute a series of promises in parallel and get all the results of each of the promises at once:

```
Promise.all([
    new Promise<number>((resolve) => {
        setTimeout(() => resolve(1), 1000);
    }),
    new Promise<number>((resolve) => {
        setTimeout(() => resolve(2), 1000);
    }),
    new Promise<number>((resolve) => {
        setTimeout(() => resolve(3), 1000);
    })
]).then((values) => {
    console.log(values); // [ 1 ,2, 3]
});
```

The `Promise` API also includes a method named `race`, which allows us to execute a series of promises in parallel and obtain the result of the first promise resolved:

```
Promise.race([
    new Promise<number>((resolve) => {
        setTimeout(() => resolve(1), 3000);
    }),
    new Promise<number>((resolve) => {
        setTimeout(() => resolve(2), 2000);
    }),
    new Promise<number>((resolve) => {
        setTimeout(() => resolve(3), 1000);
    })
]).then((fastest) => {
    console.log(fastest); // 3
});
```

We can use many different types of asynchronous flow control when working with promises:

- **Concurrent**: The tasks are executed in parallel (as in the `Promise.all` example)
- **Race**: The tasks are executed in parallel, and only the result of the fastest promise is returned

- **Series**: A group of tasks is executed in sequence, but the preceding tasks do not pass arguments to the next task
- **Waterfall**: A group of tasks is executed in sequence, and each task passes arguments to the next task (as in the example)
- **Composite**: This is any combination of the previous concurrent, series, and waterfall approaches

Covariant checking in callback parameters

TypeScript 2.4 changed the way the type system behaves internally to improve error detection in nested callbacks and promises:

- TypeScript's checking of callback parameters is now covariant in relation to immediate signature checks. Previously, it was bivariant and occasionally allowed incorrect types through.
- Basically, this means that callback parameters and classes that contain callbacks are checked more carefully, so Typescript will require stricter types in this release. This is particularly true of promises and observables due to the way in which their APIs are specified.

In TypeScript versions before 2.4, the following example was considered valid, and no errors were thrown:

```
declare function someFunc(
    callback: (
    nestedCallback: (error: number, result: any) => void
    ) => void
): void;

someFunc(
    (
        nestedCallback: (e: number) => void // Error
    ) => {
        nestedCallback(1);
    }
);
```

In TypeScript versions following the 2.4 release, we will need to add the complete signature of `nestedCallback` to resolve this error:

```
someFunc(
    (
        nestedCallback: (e: number, result: any) => void // OK
    ) => {
        nestedCallback(1, 1);
    }
);
```

Thanks to the internal change in the TypeScript type system, the following error is also detected:

```
let p: Promise<number> = new Promise((res, rej) => {
    res("error"); // Error
});
```

Before TypeScript 2.4, the preceding promise would have been inferred as `Promise<{}>` because we forgot to add the generic argument, `<number>`, when we created an instance of the `Promise` class. The string error would then have been considered a valid instance of `{}`.

> The preceding is a clear example of why it is recommended you upgrade TypeScript regularly. Each new version of TypeScript introduces new features able to detect new errors for us.

Generators

If we invoke a function in TypeScript, we can assume that, once the function starts running, it will always run to completion before any other code can run. However, one type of function known as a **generator** can may be paused in the middle of execution—once or many times—and resumed later, allowing other code to run during these paused periods.

A generator represents a sequence of values. The interface of a generator object is just an **iterator**. An iterator implements the following interface:

```
interface Iterator<T> {
    next(value?: any): IteratorResult<T>;
    return?(value?: any): IteratorResult<T>;
    throw?(e?: any): IteratorResult<T>;
}
```

The `next` function can be invoked until it runs out of values. We can define a generator by using the `function` keyword, followed by an asterisk, (*). The `yield` keyword is used to stop the execution of the function and return a value. Let's look at an example:

```
function *foo() {
    yield 1;
    yield 2;
    yield 3;
    yield 4;
    return 5;
}

let bar = foo();
bar.next(); // Object {value: 1, done: false}
bar.next(); // Object {value: 2, done: false}
bar.next(); // Object {value: 3, done: false}
bar.next(); // Object {value: 4, done: false}
bar.next(); // Object {value: 5, done: true}
bar.next(); // Object { done: true }
```

 Note that some additional types are required by generators if you are targeting ES5. You will need to add `es2015.generator` and `es2015.iterable`, and enable `downlevelIteration` to your `tsconfig.json` file:

```
"lib": [
    "es2015.promise",
    "dom",
    "es5",
    "es2015.generator", // new
    "es2015.iterable" // new
]
```

As we can see, the preceding iterator has five steps. The first time we call the `next` method, the function will be executed until it reaches the first `yield` statement, and then it will return the value 1 and stop the execution of the function until we invoke the generator's `next` method again. As we can see, we are now able to stop the function's execution at a given point. This allows us to write infinite loops without causing a stack overflow exception, as demonstrated in the following example:

```
function* foo() {
    let i = 1;
    while (true) { // Infinite loop!
        yield i++;
```

```
        }
    }

let bar = foo();
bar.next(); // Object {value: 1, done: false}
bar.next(); // Object {value: 2, done: false}
bar.next(); // Object {value: 3, done: false}
bar.next(); // Object {value: 4, done: false}
bar.next(); // Object {value: 5, done: false}
bar.next(); // Object {value: 6, done: false}
bar.next(); // Object {value: 7, done: false}
```

The generator's API opens up possibilities with reference to synchronicity, as we can call the generator's `next` method after an asynchronous event has occurred.

Asynchronous functions – async and await

Asynchronous functions are a TypeScript feature that arrived with the TypeScript 1.6 release. Developers can use the `await` keyword to wait for an asynchronous operation to be completed without blocking the normal execution of the program.

Using asynchronous functions helps to increase the readability of a piece of code when compared with the use of promises or callbacks but, technically, we can achieve the same features using both promises and asynchronous functions.

Let's take a look at a basic `async`/`await` example:

```
let p = Promise.resolve(3);

async function fn(): Promise<number> {
    var i = await p; // 3
    return 1 + i; // 4
}

fn().then((r) => console.log(r)); // 4
```

The preceding code snippet declares a promise named p. This promise represents a future result. As we can see, the `fn` function is preceded by the `async` keyword, which is used to indicate to the compiler that it is an asynchronous function.

Inside the function, the `await` keyword is used to suspend execution until the promise p is fulfilled or rejected. As we can see, the syntax is less verbose and cleaner than it would have been had we used the `Promise` API or callbacks.

An asynchronous function, such as `fn`, returns a promise at runtime. This should explain why we need to use the `then` method at the end of the code snippet.

The following code snippet showcases how we can declare an asynchronous function named `invokeTaskAsync`. The asynchronous function uses the `await` keyword to wait for the result of the `doSomethingAsync`, `doSomethingElseAsync`, and `doSomethingMoreAsync` functions that we declared during the promises example:

```
async function invokeTaskAsync() {
    let arr1 = await doSomethingAsync([]);
    let arr2 = await doSomethingElseAsync(arr1);
    return await doSomethingMoreAsync(arr2);
}
```

The `invokeTaskAsync` function is asynchronous. Therefore, it will return a promise at runtime. This means that we can use the `Promise` API to await a result or catch potential errors respectively:

```
invokeTaskAsync().then((result) => {
    console.log(
        `
        doSomethingAsync: ${result[0]}
        doSomethingElseAsync: ${result[1]}
        doSomethingMoreAsync: ${result[2]}
        `
    );
}).catch((e) => {
    console.log(e);
});
```

We can also define asynchronous IIFE as a convenient way to use the `async` and `await` keywords:

```
(async () => {
    try {
        let arr1 = await doSomethingAsync([]);
        let arr2 = await doSomethingElseAsync(arr1);
        let arr3 = await doSomethingMoreAsync(arr2);
        console.log(
            `
            doSomethingAsync: ${arr3[0]}
            doSomethingElseAsync: ${arr3[1]}
            doSomethingMoreAsync: ${arr3[2]}
            `
        );
    } catch (e) {
        console.log(e);
```

```
    }
})();
```

Using an `async` IIFE is very useful because it is very common to not be able to use the `await` keyword outside a function, for example, in the entry point of an application. We can use the `async` IIFE to overcome this limitation:

```
(async () => {
    await someAsyncFunction();
})();
```

Asynchronous generators

We have already learned about the interface implemented by all iterators:

```
interface Iterator<T> {
  next(value?: any): IteratorResult<T>;
  return?(value?: any): IteratorResult<T>;
  throw?(e?: any): IteratorResult<T>;
}
```

However, we haven't learned yet about the interface implemented by all asynchronous iterators:

```
interface AsyncIterator<T> {
  next(value?: any): Promise<IteratorResult<T>>;
  return?(value?: any): Promise<IteratorResult<T>>;
  throw?(e?: any): Promise<IteratorResult<T>>;
}
```

An asynchronous iterator returns a promise every time we invoke the `next` method. The following code snippet demonstrates how asynchronous iterators can be very useful when used in conjunction with asynchronous functions:

```
let counter = 0;

function doSomethingAsync() {
    return new Promise<number>((r) => {
        setTimeout(() => {
            counter += 1;
            r(counter);
        }, 1000);
    });
}

async function* g1() {
```

```
    yield await doSomethingAsync();
    yield await doSomethingAsync();
    yield await doSomethingAsync();
}

let i: AsyncIterableIterator<number> = g1();
i.next().then((n) => console.log(n)); // 1
i.next().then((n) => console.log(n)); // 2
i.next().then((n) => console.log(n)); // 3
```

Some additional types are required by asynchronous iterators if we are targeting ES5. You will need to add `esnext.asynciterable` and enable `downlevelIteration` in your `tsconfig.json` file. We are also going to need to enable an additional setting in our `tsconfig.json` to provide full support for iterables in `for-of`, spread, and destructuring when targeting ES5 or ES3:

```
"lib": [
    "es2015.promise",
    "dom",
    "es5",
    "es2015.generator",
    "es2015.iterable",
    "esnext.asynciterable" // new
]
```

Asynchronous iteration (for await...of)

We can use the new `await...of` expression to iterate and await each of the promises returned by an asynchronous iterator:

```
function* g1() {
    yield 2;
    yield 3;
    yield 4;
}

async function func() {
    for await (const x of g1()) {
        console.log(x);
    }
}

(async () => {
```

```
        await func();
})();
```

Delegating to another generator (yield*)

We can use the `yield*` expression to delegate from one generator to another. The following code snippet defines two generator functions, named `g1` and `g2`. The `g2` generator uses the `yield*` expression to delegate the iteration to the iterator created by `g1`:

```
function* g1() {
    yield 2;
    yield 3;
    yield 4;
}

function* g2() {
    yield 1;
    yield* g1();
    yield 5;
}

var iterator1 = g2();

console.log(iterator1.next()); // {value: 1, done: false}
console.log(iterator1.next()); // {value: 2, done: false}
console.log(iterator1.next()); // {value: 3, done: false}
console.log(iterator1.next()); // {value: 4, done: false}
console.log(iterator1.next()); // {value: 5, done: false}
console.log(iterator1.next()); // {value: undefined, done: true}
```

The `yield*` expression can also be used to delegate the iteration to some *iterables*, such as arrays:

```
function* g2() {
    yield 1;
    yield* [2, 3, 4];
    yield 5;
}

var iterator = g2();

console.log(iterator.next()); // {value: 1, done: false}
console.log(iterator.next()); // {value: 2, done: false}
console.log(iterator.next()); // {value: 3, done: false}
console.log(iterator.next()); // {value: 4, done: false}
console.log(iterator.next()); // {value: 5, done: false}
console.log(iterator.next()); // {value: undefined, done: true}
```

 Please note that the preceding example requires a number of particular settings in the `tsconfig.json` file. Please refer to the preceding notes in this chapter to learn more about the required settings.

Summary

In this chapter, we have focused on the use of callbacks, promises, and generators to take advantage of the asynchronous programming capabilities of TypeScript. In the next chapter, we will look at the runtime to understand how the event loop and the `this` operator work. These concepts will help us to understand some of the implementations of functional programming techniques that we will explore later in this book.

The Runtime – The Event Loop and the this Operator

Over the next two chapters, we are going to learn about some concepts that are closely related to the TypeScript runtime. TypeScript is only used at design time; the TypeScript code is then compiled into JavaScript and finally executed at runtime. The JavaScript runtime oversees the execution of the JavaScript code. It is essential to understand that we will never execute TypeScript code and we will always execute JavaScript code; for this reason, when we refer to the TypeScript runtime, we will, in fact, be talking about the JavaScript runtime.

Understanding the runtime is crucial because it will help us to understand the implementation of a number of functional programming techniques that we will explore later in this book.

In this chapter, we will cover the following topics:

- The environment
- The `event` loop
- The `this` operator

Let's start by learning about the environment.

The environment

The runtime environment is one of the first things that we must think about before we can start developing a TypeScript application. Once we have compiled our TypeScript code into JavaScript, it can be executed in many different environments. While most of those environments will be part of a web browser such as Chrome, Internet Explorer, or Firefox, we might also want to be able to run our code on the server side or, in a desktop application, in environments such as Node.js, RingoJS, or Electron.

It is essential to keep in mind that there are some variables and objects available at runtime that are environment-specific. For example, we could create a library and access the `document.layers` variable. While `document` is part of the W3C **Document Object Model** (**DOM**) standard, the `layers` property is only available in Internet Explorer and is not part of the W3C DOM standard.

The *W3C* defines the DOM as:

> *The Document Object Model is a platform- and language-neutral interface that will allow programs and scripts to dynamically access and update the content, structure, and style of documents. The document can be further processed, and the results of that processing can be incorporated back into the presented page.*

Similarly, we can also access a set of objects known as the **Browser Object Model** (**BOM**) from a web browser runtime environment. The BOM consists of the `navigator`, `history`, `screen`, `location`, and `document` objects, which are properties of the `window` object.

We need to keep in mind that the DOM is only available in web browsers. If we want to run our application in a web browser, we will be able to access the DOM and BOM. However, in environments such as Node.js or RingoJS, these APIs will not be available since they are standalone JavaScript environments completely independent of a web browser. We can also find other objects in the server-side environments (such as `process.stdin` in Node.js) that will not be available if we attempt to execute our code in a web browser.

We also need to keep in mind the existence of multiple versions of these JavaScript environments. In some cases, we will have to support multiple browsers and various versions of Node.js. The recommended practice when dealing with this problem is to use conditional statements that check for the availability of features:

```
if (Promise && typeof Promise.all === "function") {
    // User Promise.all here...
}
```

This is executed instead of checking the availability of an environment or version:

```
if (
    navigator.userAgent.toLowerCase().indexOf('chrome') > -1 &&
    navigator.vendor.toLowerCase().indexOf("google") > -1
) {
    // Use Promise.all here...
}
```

 An excellent library is available that can help us to implement feature detection when developing for web browsers. The library is called **Modernizr**, and can be downloaded at `http://modernizr.com/`.

Understanding the event loop

The TypeScript runtime (JavaScript) has a concurrency model based on an `event` loop. This model is quite different from the model in other languages, such as C or Java. Before focusing on the `event` loop itself, we must first understand a number of runtime concepts.

What follows is a visual representation of some critical runtime concepts: **HEAP**, **STACK**, **QUEUE**, and **FRAME**:

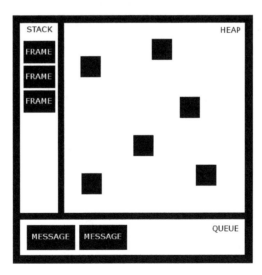

We will now look at the role of each of these runtime concepts.

Frames

A **frame** is a sequential unit of work. In the preceding diagram, frames are represented by the blocks inside the stack.

When a `function` is invoked in JavaScript, the runtime creates a frame in the stack. The frame holds that function's arguments and local variables. When the function returns, the frame is removed from the stack. Let's look at an example:

```
function foo(a: number): number {
    const localFooValue = 12;
    return localFooValue + a;
}

function bar(b: number): number {
    const localBarValue = 4;
    return foo(localBarValue * b);
}
```

After declaring the `foo` and `bar` functions, we invoke the `bar` function:

```
bar(21);
```

When the `bar` function is executed, the runtime will create a new frame containing the arguments of `bar` and all its local variables (`b` and `localBarValue`). The frame (represented as a black square in the preceding diagram) is then added to the top of the stack.

Internally, the `bar` function invokes the `foo` function. When `foo` is invoked, a new frame is created and allocated to the top of the stack. When the execution of `foo` is finished (`foo` has returned), the top frame is removed from the stack. When the execution of `bar` is also completed, it is removed from the stack as well.

Now, let's imagine what would happen if the `foo` function invoked the `bar` function:

```
function foo(a: number): number {
    const localFooValue = 12;
    return bar(localFooValue + a);
}

function bar(b: number): number {
    const localBarValue = 4;
    return foo(localBarValue * b);
}
```

The preceding code snippet creates a never-ending `function call` loop. With each function call, a new frame is added to the stack, and eventually there will be no more space in the stack and an error will be thrown. Most software engineers are familiar with this error, known as a **stack overflow** error.

Stack

The **stack** contains sequential steps (frames). A stack is a data structure that represents a simple **Last-in-first-out** (**LIFO**) collection of objects. Therefore, when a frame is added to the stack, it is always added to the top of the stack.

Since the stack is a LIFO collection, the `event` loop processes the frames stored in it from top to bottom. The dependencies of a frame are added to the top of it in the stack to ensure that all the dependencies of each of the frames are met.

Queue

The **queue** contains a list of waiting to be processed. Each is associated with a function. When the stack is empty, a message is taken out of the queue and processed. The processing consists of calling the associated function and adding the frames to the stack. Message processing ends when the stack becomes empty again.

In the previous runtime diagram, the blocks inside the queue represent the messages. The messages are usually generated by user or applications events. For example, when the user clicks in an element with an event handler, a new message is added to the queue.

Heap

The **heap** is a memory container that is not aware of the order of the items stored in it. The heap contains all the variables and objects currently in use. It may also contain frames that are currently out of scope but have not yet been removed from the memory by the garbage collector.

The event loop

Concurrency is the ability to execute two or more operations simultaneously. The JavaScript runtime execution takes place on a single thread, which means that we cannot achieve real concurrency.

The **event loop** follows a run-to-completion approach, which means that it will process a message from beginning to end before any other message is processed.

 As we saw in `Chapter 3`, *Mastering Asynchronous Programming*, we can use the `yield` keyword and generators to pause the execution of a function.

Every time a function is invoked, a new message is added to the queue. If the stack is empty, the function is processed (the frames are added to the stack).

When all the frames have been added to the stack, the stack is cleared from top to bottom. At the end of the process, the stack is empty, and the next message is processed.

 Web workers can perform background tasks in a different thread. They have their queue, heap, and stack.

One of the advantages of the `event` loop is that the execution order is quite predictable and easy to follow. A disadvantage of this approach is that, if a message takes too long to complete, the application becomes unresponsive. A good practice to follow is to make message processing short and, if possible, split one message into several messages.

 The Node.js runtime features a non-blocking I/O model in combination with a single-thread event loop model, which means that, when the application is waiting for an I/O operation to finish, it can still process other things, such as user input.

The this operator

In JavaScript, the `this` operator behaves a little differently compared to other languages. The value of the `this` operator is often determined by the way a function is invoked. Its value cannot be set by assignment during execution, and it may be different each time a function is invoked.

 The `this` operator also has some differences when using **strict** and **non-strict** modes. ECMAScript 5's strict mode is a way to opt into a restricted variant of JavaScript. You can learn more about strict mode at `https://developer.mozilla.org/en-US/docs/Web/JavaScript/Reference/Strict_mode`.

The this operator in the global context

In the global context, the `this` operator will always point to the global object. In a web browser, the `window` object is the global object:

```
console.log(this === window); // true
this.a = 37;
console.log(window.a); // 37
console.log(window.document === this.document); // true
console.log(this.document === document); // true
console.log(window.document === document); // true
```

The preceding example should be implemented using JavaScript. The preceding code will fail in TypeScript if the `strict` compilation flag is enabled because the `strict` flag enables the `noImplicitThis` flag, which prevents us from using the `this` operator in a scope in which its value is not clear, such as a global scope.

The this operator in the function context

The value of `this` inside a function depends on how the function is invoked. If we invoke a function in non-strict mode, the value of `this` within the function will point to the global object:

```
function f1() {
  return this;
}

f1() === window; // true
```

The preceding example should be implemented using JavaScript. The preceding code will fail in TypeScript when the `strict` compilation flag is enabled because it also enables the `noImplicitThis` flag.

However, if we invoke a function in strict mode, the value of `this` within the function's body will be `undefined`:

```
console.log(this); // global (window)

function f2() {
  "use strict";
  return this; // undefined
```

```
}

console.log(f2()); // undefined
console.log(this); // window
```

 The preceding example should be implemented using JavaScript.

However, the value of the this operator inside a function invoked as an instance method points to the instance. In other words, the value of the this operator within a function that is part of a class (a method) points to the class instance:

```
const person = {
  age: 37,
  getAge: function() {
    return this.age; // this points to the instance (person)
  }
};

console.log(person.getAge()); // 37
```

 The preceding example should be implemented using JavaScript.

In the preceding example, we have used object literal notation to define an object named person, but the same applies when declaring objects using classes:

```
class Person {
  public age: number;
  public constructor(age: number) {
    this.age = age;
  }
  public getAge() {
    return this.age; // this points to the instance (person)
  }
}

const person = new Person(37);
console.log(person.getAge()); // 37
```

The preceding example should be implemented using TypeScript.

At runtime, classes are implemented (using what are known as prototypes) as a prototype chain. Don't worry if you don't know much about prototypes because we will learn more about them in the next chapter. All we need to know for now is that the behavior described in the preceding section takes place when working with prototypes:

```
function Person(age) {
    this.age = age;
}

Person.prototype.getAge = function () {
    return this.age; // this points to the instance (person)
};

var person = new Person(37);
console.log(person.getAge()); // 37
```

 The preceding example should be implemented using JavaScript.

When a function is used as a constructor (with the new keyword), the this operator points to the object being constructed:

```
function Person() { // function used as a constructor
  this.age = 37;
}

const person = new Person();
console.log(person.age); // logs 37
```

 The preceding example should be implemented using JavaScript.

The call, apply, and bind methods

All functions inherit the `call`, `apply`, and `bind` methods from `Function.prototype`. We can use these methods to set the value of `this`.

The `call` and `apply` methods are almost identical; both methods allow us to invoke a function and set the value of the `this` operator within the function. The main difference between `call` and `apply` is that, while `apply` lets us invoke the function with arguments as an array, `call` requires that function parameters be listed explicitly.

A useful mnemonic is A (apply) for an array and C (call) for a comma.

Let's look at an example. We will start by declaring a class named `Person`. This class has two properties (`name` and `surname`) and one method (`greet`). The `greet` method uses the `this` operator to access the `name` and `surname` instance properties:

```
class Person {

    public name: string;
    public surname: string;

    public constructor(name: string, surname: string) {
        this.name = name;
        this.surname = surname;
    }

    public greet(city: string, country: string) {
        // we use the this operator to access name and surname
        let msg = `Hi, my name is ${this.name} ${this.surname}.`;
        msg += `I'm from ${city} (${country}).`;
        console.log(msg);
    }

}
```

After declaring the `Person` class, we will create an instance:

```
const person = new Person("remo", "Jansen");
```

If we invoke the `greet` method, it will work as expected:

```
person.greet("Seville", "Spain");
```

Alternatively, we can invoke the method using the `call` and `apply` functions. We have supplied the `person` object as the first parameter of both functions because we want the `this` operator (inside the `greet` method) to take `person` as its value:

```
person.greet.call(person, "Seville", "Spain");
person.greet.apply(person, ["Seville", "Spain"]);
```

If we provide a different value to be used as the value of `this`, we will not be able to access the `name` and `surname` properties within the `greet` function:

```
person.greet.call(null, "Seville", "Spain");
person.greet.apply(null, ["Seville", "Spain"]);
```

The two preceding examples may seem useless because the first one invoked the function directly and the second one caused unexpected behavior. The `apply` and `call` methods only make sense when we want the `this` operator to take a different value when a function is invoked:

```
const valueOfThis = { name : "Anakin", surname : "Skywalker" };
person.greet.call(valueOfThis, "Mos espa", "Tatooine");
person.greet.apply(valueOfThis, ["Mos espa", "Tatooine"]);
```

The `bind` method can be used to set the value of the `this` operator (within a function), regardless of how it is invoked.

When we invoke a function's `bind` method, it returns a new function with the same body and scope as the original function, but the `this` operator (within the body function) is permanently bound to the first argument of `bind`, regardless of how the function is being used.

Let's look at an example. We will start by creating an instance of the `Person` class that we declared in the previous example:

```
const person = new Person("Remo", "Jansen");
```

Then we can use `bind` to set the `greet` function as a new function with the same scope and body:

```
const greet = person.greet.bind(person);
```

If we try to invoke the `greet` function using `bind` and `apply`, just like we did in the previous example, we will be able to observe that, this time, the `this` operator will always point to the object instance, irrespective of how the function is invoked:

```
greet.call(person, "Seville", "Spain");
greet.apply(person, ["Seville", "Spain"]);
// Hi, my name is Remo Jansen. I'm from Seville Spain.

greet.call(null, "Seville", "Spain");
greet.apply(null, ["Seville", "Spain"]);
// Hi, my name is Remo Jansen. I'm from Seville Spain.

const valueOfThis = { name: "Anakin", surname: "Skywalker" };
greet.call(valueOfThis, "Mos espa", "Tatooine");
greet.apply(valueOfThis, ["Mos espa", "Tatooine"]);
// Hi, my name is Remo Jansen. I'm from Mos espa Tatooine.
```

 Using the `apply`, `call`, and `bind` methods is not recommended unless you are very familiar with what you are doing, because they can result in other developers encountering complex and hard-to-debug runtime issues.

Once we bind an object to a function with `bind`, we cannot override it:

```
const valueOfThis = { name: "Anakin", surname: "Skywalker" };
const greet = person.greet.bind(valueOfThis);
greet.call(valueOfThis, "Mos espa", "Tatooine");
greet.apply(valueOfThis, ["Mos espa", "Tatooine"]);
// Hi, my name is Remo Jansen. I'm from Mos espa Tatooine.
```

 The use of `bind`, `apply`, and `call` is discouraged in JavaScript because it can lead to confusion. Modifying the default behavior of the `this` operator can lead to unexpected results. Remember to use these methods only when strictly necessary and to document your code correctly to reduce the risk caused by potential maintainability issues. However, TypeScript 3.2.0 introduces a new compilation flag, known as `strictBindCallApply`, that makes the `bind`, `apply`, and `call` methods safer.

Summary

In this chapter, we have learned some fundamental aspects of the TypeScript and JavaScript runtime. We have learned that a potential differences lies in the execution environments of web browsers and platforms such as Node.js. We have also learned the functions are processed and executed by the `event` loop and how the value of the `this` operator can change in different contexts.

In the next chapter, we will learn more about the runtime, and we will explore closures and prototypes. We will then be fully ready to delve into the implementation of a wide variety of functional programming techniques.

5
The Runtime – Closures and Prototypes

In the previous chapter, we learned about certain aspects of the TypeScript/JavaScript runtime that will help us to understand the implementation of some functional programming techniques in upcoming chapters. In this chapter, we are going to explore two more aspects of the TypeScript/JavaScript runtime:

- Prototypes
- Closures

After exploring these two concepts, we will finally be ready to delve into the implementation and application of the main functional programming techniques.

Prototypes

When we compile a TypeScript program, all classes and objects become JavaScript objects. Occasionally, however, we may encounter an unexpected behavior at runtime even if the compilation was completed without errors. To be able to identify and understand the cause of this behavior, we need a good understanding of the JavaScript runtime. One of the main concepts that we need to understand is how classes and inheritance work at runtime.

The runtime inheritance system uses a prototypal inheritance model. In a prototypal inheritance model, objects inherit from objects, and there are no classes available. However, we can use prototypes to simulate classes. Let's see how this works.

At runtime, objects have an internal property called `prototype`. The values of the `prototype` property is an object that contains some properties (data) and methods (behavior).

In TypeScript, we can use a class-based inheritance system:

```
class Person {

    public name: string;
    public surname: string;
    public age: number = 0;

    public constructor(name: string, surname: string) {
        this.name = name;
        this.surname = surname;
    }

    public greet() {
        let msg = 'Hi! my name is ${this.name} ${this.surname}';
        msg += 'I'm ${this.age}';
    }

}
```

We have defined a class named `Person`. At runtime, this class is declared using prototypes instead of classes:

```
var Person = (function() {

    function Person(name, surname) {
        this.age = 0;
        this.name = name;
        this.surname = surname;
    }

    Person.prototype.greet = function() {
        let msg = "Hi! my name is " + this.name +
                    " " + this.surname;
        msg += "I'm " + this.age;
    };

    return Person;

})();
```

The preceding code is emitted by TypeScript when we target ES5. The `class` keyword is supported by ES6 at runtime, but it is only syntactic sugar.

Syntactic sugar is syntax within a programming language that is designed to make things easier to read or to express. This means that the class keyword is just a helper to make our lives as software engineers easier; internally, prototypes are always used.

The TypeScript compiler wraps the object definition (we will not refer to it as a class definition because technically, it is not a class) with an **immediately-invoked function expression** (**IIFE**). Inside the IIFE, we can find a function named `Person`. If we examine the function and compare it with the TypeScript class, we will notice that it takes the same parameters that the class constructor takes in the TypeScript class. This function is used to create new instances of the `Person` class.

After the constructor, we can see the definition of the `greet` method. As we can see, the `prototype` property is used to attach the `greet` method to the `Person` class.

Instance properties versus class properties

Because JavaScript is a dynamic programming language, we can add properties and methods to an instance of an object at runtime; and they don't need to be part of the object (class) itself:

```
const name = "Remo";
const surname = "Jansen";

function Person(name, surname) {
     // instance properties
     this.name = name;
     this.surname = surname;
}

const person1 = new Person(name, surname);
person1.age = 27;
```

We have defined a constructor function for an object named `Person`, which takes two variables (`name` and `surname`) as arguments. Then we have created an instance of the `Person` object and added a new property named `age` to it. We can use a `for...in` statement to check the properties of `person1` at runtime:

```
for(let property in person1) {
   console.log("property: " + property + ", value: '" +
   person1[property] + "'");
}
```

The following will be displayed in the console output:

```
property: name, value: 'Remo'
property: surname, value: 'Jansen'
property: age, value: 27
property: greet, value: 'function (city, country) {
    let msg = "Hi, my name is " + this.name + " " + this.surname;
    msg += "\nI'm from " + city + " " + country;
    console.log(msg);
}'
```

As we can see, `age` has been added as a property. All these properties are instance properties because they hold a value for each new instance. If, for example, we create a new instance of `Person`, both instances will hold their own values:

```
let person2 = new Person("John", "Wick");
person2.name; // "John"
person1.name; // "Remo"
```

We have defined these instance properties using the `this` operator because, when a function is used as a constructor (with the `new` keyword), the `this` operator is bound to the object instance constructed. The preceding also explains why we can alternatively define instance properties through the object's prototype:

```
Person.prototype.name = name; // instance property
Person.prototype.surname = surname; // instance property
```

We can also declare class properties and methods (also known as static properties). The main difference between instance properties and class properties is that the value of class properties and methods are shared between all instances of an object. Class properties are often used to store static values:

```
function MathHelper() {
  //...
}

// class property
MathHelper.PI = 3.14159265359;
```

Class methods are also often used as utility functions that perform calculations on supplied parameters and return a result:

```
function MathHelper() {
    // ...
}

// class property
```

```
MathHelper.PI = 3.14159265359;

// class method
MathHelper.areaOfCircle = function(radius) {
  return radius * radius * MathHelper.PI;
}
```

 Please note that the preceding code snippet is valid in JavaScript, but will throw a compilation error in TypeScript.

In the preceding example, we accessed a class attribute (PI) from a class method (areaOfCircle). We can access class properties from instance methods, but we cannot access instance properties or methods from class properties or methods. We can demonstrate this by declaring PI as an instance property instead of a class property:

```
function MathHelper() {
  // instance property
  this.PI = 3.14159265359;
}
```

If we then attempt to access PI from a class method, it will be undefined:

```
// class method
MathHelper.areaOfCircle = function(radius) {
  return radius * radius * this.PI; // this.PI is undefined
}

MathHelper.areaOfCircle(5); // NaN
```

We are not supposed to access class methods or properties from instance methods, but there is a way to do it. We can do this by using the prototype's constructor property, as demonstrated in the following example:

```
function MathHelper () { /* ... */ }

// class property
MathHelper.PI = 3.14159265359;

// instance method
MathHelper.prototype.areaOfCircle = function(radius) {
 return radius * radius * this.constructor.PI;
}

const math = new MathHelper ();
console.log(MathHelper.areaOfCircle(5)); // 78.53981633975
```

We can access the PI class property from the areaOfCircle instance method using the prototype's constructor property because this property returns a reference to the object's constructor.

Inside areaOfCircle, the this operator returns a reference to the object's prototype:

```
this === MathHelper.prototype; // true
```

We may deduce that this.constructor is equal to MathHelper.prototype.constructor and, therefore, MathHelper.prototype.constructor is equal to MathHelper.

In TypeScript, we can define class properties using the static keyword:

```
class MathHelper {

    // class property
    public static PI = 3.14159265359;

    // class method
    public static areaOfCircle(radius: number) {
        return radius * radius * MathHelper.PI;
    }
}
```

Prototypal inheritance

You might be wondering how the extends keyword works. Let's create a new TypeScript class, which inherits from the Person class, to understand it:

```
class SuperHero extends Person {

    public superpower: string;

    public constructor(
        name: string,
        surname: string,
        superpower: string
    ) {
        super(name, surname);
        this.superpower = superpower;
    }

    public userSuperPower() {
        return 'I'm using my ${this.superpower}';
```

```
      }

  }
```

The preceding class is named `SuperHero` and extends the `Person` class. It has one additional attribute (`superpower`) and method (`useSuperPower`).

We need to compile the previous code snippet into JavaScript code so we can examine how inheritance is implemented at runtime. The compiler will generate a polyfill function named `__extends` which is meant to be a replacement for the extends keyword compatible with the older versions of JavaScript:

```
var __extends = this.__extends || function (d, b) {
    for (var p in b) if (b.hasOwnProperty(p)) d[p] = b[p];
    function __() { this.constructor = d; }
    __.prototype = b.prototype;
    d.prototype = new __();
};
```

Please note that the preceding code snippet is slightly more complicated in the latest version of TypeScript. We will use the code from previous versions here because it contains fewer conditions and is easier to understand.

This piece of code is generated by TypeScript. Even though it is a small piece of code, it showcases almost every concept contained in this chapter, and understanding it can be quite challenging.

Before the function expression is evaluated for the first time, the `this` operator points to the global object, which does not contain a method named `__extends`. This means that the `__extends` variable is undefined.

When the function expression is evaluated for the first time, the value of the function expression (an anonymous function) is assigned to the `__extends` property in the global scope.

TypeScript generates the function expression on one occasion for each TypeScript file containing the `extends` keyword. However, the function expression is only evaluated once (when the `__extends` variable is undefined). This behavior is implemented by the conditional statement in the first line:

```
var __extends = this.__extends || function (d, b) { // ...
```

The first time the preceding line of code is executed, the function expression is evaluated.

The value of the function expression is an anonymous function, which is assigned to the __extends variable in the global scope. Because we are in the global scope, var __extends and this. __extends refer to the same variable at this point.

When a new file is executed, the __extends variable is already available in the global scope, and the function expression is not evaluated. This means that the value of the function expression is only assigned to the __extends variable once, even if the snippet is executed multiple times.

Let's focus now on the __extends variable (the anonymous function):

```
function (d, b) {
    for (var p in b) if (b.hasOwnProperty(p)) d[p] = b[p];
    function __() { this.constructor = d; }
    __.prototype = b.prototype;
    d.prototype = new __();
}
```

This function takes two arguments named d and b. When we invoke it, we should pass a derived object constructor (d) and a base object constructor (b).

The first line inside the anonymous function iterates each class property and method from the base class and creates their copy in the derived class:

```
for (var p in b) if (b.hasOwnProperty(p)) d[p] = b[p];
```

 When we use a for...in statement to iterate an instance of an object to a, it will iterate the object's instance properties. However, if we use a for...in statement to iterate the properties of an object's constructor, the statement will iterate its class properties. In the preceding example, the for...in statement is used to inherit the object's class properties and methods. To inherit the instance properties, we will copy the object's prototype.

The second line declares a new constructor function named __ and, inside it, the this operator is used to access its prototype.

```
function __() { this.constructor = d; }
```

The prototype contains a special property named constructor, which returns a reference to the object's constructor. The function named __ and this.constructor are pointing to the same variable at this point. The value of the derived object constructor (d) is then assigned to the __ constructor.

In the third line, the value of the prototype object from the base object constructor is assigned to the prototype of the __ object constructor:

```
__.prototype = b.prototype;
```

In the last line, the __ function is invoked as a constructor with the new keyword, and the result is assigned to the derived class (d) prototype. By performing all these steps, we have achieved what we need to in order to invoke the following:

```
var instance = new d():
```

Upon doing so, we will get an object that contains all the properties from both the derived class (d) and the base class (b). Furthermore, any instance objects constructed by the derived constructor (d) will be instances of the derived class, while inheriting the class and instance properties and methods from the base class (b).

We can see the function in action by examining the runtime code that defines the SuperHero class:

```
var SuperHero = (function (_super) {

    __extends(SuperHero, _super);

    function SuperHero(name, surname, superpower) {
        _super.call(this, name, surname);
        this.superpower = superpower;
    }

    SuperHero.prototype.userSuperPower = function () {
        return "I'm using my " + superpower;
    };

    return SuperHero;

}) (Person);
```

We can see an IIFE here again. This time, the IIFE takes the Person object constructor as the argument. Inside the function, we will refer to this argument using the name _super. Inside the IIFE, the __extends function is invoked and the SuperHero (derived class) and _super (base class) arguments are passed to it.

In the next line, we can find the declaration of the SuperHero object constructor and the useSuperPower function. We can use SuperHero as an argument of __extend before it is declared because function declarations are hoisted to the top of the scope.

Function expressions are not hoisted. When we assign a function to a variable in a function expression, the variable is hoisted, but its value (the function itself) is not hoisted.

Inside the `SuperHero` constructor, the base class (`Person`) constructor is invoked using the `call` method:

```
_super.call(this, name, surname);
```

As we discovered in the previous chapter, we can use `call` to set the value of the `this` operator in a function context. In this case, we are passing the `this` operator, which points to the instance of `SuperHero` being created:

```
function Person(name, surname) {
    // this points to the instance of SuperHero being created
    this.name = name;
    this.surname = surname;
}
```

Prototype chains and property shadowing

When we try to access a property or a method of an object, the runtime will search for that property or method in the object's own properties and methods. If it is not found, the runtime will continue searching through the object's inherited properties by navigating the entire inheritance tree. Because a derived object is linked to its base object through the `prototype` property, we refer to this inheritance tree as the **prototype chain**.

Let's look at an example. We will declare two simple TypeScript classes, named `Base` and `Derived`:

```
class Base {
    public method1() { return 1; }
    public method2() { return 2; }
}

class Derived extends Base {
    public method2() { return 3; }
    public method3() { return 4; }
}
```

Now we will examine the JavaScript code generated by TypeScript:

```
var Base = (function () {
    function Base() {
    }
    Base.prototype.method1 = function () { return 1; };
    Base.prototype.method2 = function () { return 2; };
    return Base;
})();

var Derived = (function (_super) {
    __extends(Derived, _super);
    function Derived() {
        _super.apply(this, arguments);
    }
    Derived.prototype.method2 = function () { return 3; };
    Derived.prototype.method3 = function () { return 4; };
    return Derived;
})(Base);
```

We can then create an instance of the `Derived` class:

```
const derived = new Derived();
```

The `new` operator creates an object instance that inherits from the `Base` class.

If we try to access the method named `method1`, the runtime will find it in the instance's properties:

```
console.log(derived.method1()); // 1
```

The instance also has its own property named `method2` (with a value of 2), but there is also an inherited property named `method2` (with a value of 3). The object's property (`method2` with a value of 3) prevents access to the prototype property (`method2` with a value of 2). This is known as **property shadowing**:

```
console.log(derived.method2()); // 3
```

The instance does not have its own property named `method3`, but it does have a property named `method3` in its prototype chain:

```
console.log(derived.method3()); // 4
```

Neither the instance nor the objects in the prototype chain (the `Base` class) have a property named `method4`:

```
console.log(derived.method4()); // error
```

Accessing the prototype of an object

Prototypes can be accessed in three different ways:

- `Person.prototype`
- `Object.getPrototypeOf(person)`
- `person.__proto__`

 The use of __proto__ is controversial and has been discouraged by many experienced software engineers. It was never originally included in the ECMAScript language specification, but modern browsers decided to implement it in any case. Today, the __proto__ property has been standardized in the ECMAScript 6 language specification and will be supported in future, but it is still a slow operation that should be avoided if performance is a concern.

Closures

Closures are one of the most powerful features in JavaScript and TypeScript, but they are also one of the most misunderstood. The *Mozilla developer network* defines closures as follows:

> *Closures are functions that refer to independent (free) variables. In other words, the function defined in the closure 'remembers' the environment in which it was created.*

We understand independent (free) variables as variables that persist beyond the lexical scope from which they were created. Let's look at an example:

```
function makeArmy() {
    const shooters = [];
    for (let i = 0; i < 10; i++) {
        const shooter = () => { // a shooter is a function
            console.log(i); // which should display it's number
        };
        shooters.push(shooter);
    }
    return shooters;
}
```

Please note that the preceding example is meant to be a JavaScript example.

We have declared a function named `makeArmy`. Inside the function, we have created an array of functions named `shooters`. Each function in the `shooters` array will display a number, the value of which was set from the variable i inside a `for` statement. We will now invoke the `makeArmy` function:

```
const army = makeArmy();
```

The `army` variable should now contain the array of the function's `shooters`. However, we will notice a problem if we execute the following piece of code:

```
army[0](); // 10 (expected 0)
army[5](); // 10 (expected 5)
```

The preceding code snippet does not work as expected because we made one of the most common mistakes related to closures. When we declared the `shooter` function inside the `makeArmy` function, we created a closure without being aware of it.

This is because the functions assigned to `shooter` are closures. A closure has access to variables in the environment that encloses them (the `makeArmy` function's scope). Ten closure functions have been created, but each one shares the same single environment. By the time the `shooter` functions are executed, the loop has run its course and the i variable (shared by all the closure functions) has been left pointing to the last entry (10).

One solution, in this case, is to use more closures:

```
function makeArmy() {
    const shooters = [];
    for (let i = 0; i < 10; i++) {
        ((index: number) => {
            const shooter = () => {
                console.log(index);
            };
            shooters.push(shooter);
        })(i);
    }
    return shooters;
}

const army = makeArmy();
army[0](); // 0
army[5](); // 5
```

Please note that the preceding example is meant to be a TypeScript example.

This works as expected. Rather than the `shooter` functions sharing a single environment, the immediately-invoked function creates a new environment for each one in which `i` refers to the corresponding value.

Static variables powered by closures

In the previous section, we learned that, when a variable in a closure context can be shared between multiple instances of a class, this means that the variable behaves like a static variable. We will now see how we can create variables and methods that behave like a static variable using closures. Let's start by declaring a TypeScript class named `Counter`:

```typescript
class Counter {

private static _COUNTER = 0;

public increment() {
this._changeBy(1);
}

public decrement() {
this._changeBy(-1);
}

public value() {
return Counter._COUNTER;
}

private _changeBy(val: number) {
Counter._COUNTER += val;
}

}
```

Please note that the preceding example is meant to be a TypeScript example.

The preceding class contains a static member named _COUNTER. The TypeScript compiler transforms it into the following code:

```
var Counter = (function () {

    function Counter() {
    }

    Counter.prototype._changeBy = function (val) {
        Counter._COUNTER += val;
    };

    Counter.prototype.increment = function () {
        this._changeBy(1);
    };

    Counter.prototype.decrement = function () {
        this._changeBy(-1);
    };

    Counter.prototype.value = function () {
        return Counter._COUNTER;
    };

    Counter._COUNTER = 0;
    return Counter;

})();
```

 Please note that the preceding code snippet is the compilation output generated by the TypeScript compiler.

As we can observe, the static variable is declared by the TypeScript compiler as a class property (as opposed to an instance property). The compiler uses a class property because class properties are shared across all instances of a class. The problem is that the private variable is not private at runtime.

Alternatively, we could write some JavaScript (remember that all valid JavaScript is valid TypeScript) code to emulate static properties using closures:

```
var Counter = (function() {

    // closure context

    let _COUNTER = 0;
```

```
function changeBy(val: number) {
    _COUNTER += val;
}

interface Counter {
    increment: () => void;
    decrement: () => void;
    value: () => number;
}

interface CounterConstructor {
    new(): Counter;
}

function Counter() {};

// closure functions

Counter.prototype.increment = function() {
    changeBy(1);
};

Counter.prototype.decrement = function() {
    changeBy(-1);
};

Counter.prototype.value = function() {
    return _COUNTER;
};

return (Counter as unknown) as CounterConstructor;

})();
```

 Please note that the preceding example is meant to be a TypeScript example.

The preceding code snippet declares a class named `Counter`. The class has some methods used to increment, decrement, and read the variable named _COUNTER. The _COUNTER variable itself is not part of the object prototype.

All the instances of the `Counter` class will share the same context, which means that the context (the _COUNTER variable and the `changeBy` function) will behave as a singleton.

The singleton pattern requires an object to be declared as a static variable to avoid the need to create its instance whenever it is required. The object instance is, therefore, shared by all the components in the application. The singleton pattern is frequently used in scenarios where it is not beneficial, thereby introducing unnecessary restrictions in situations where a unique instance of a class is not required, and introduces global state into an application.

So now we know that it is possible to use closures to emulate static variables:

```
let counter1 = new Counter();
let counter2 = new Counter();
console.log(counter1.value()); // 0
console.log(counter2.value()); // 0
counter1.increment();
counter1.increment();
console.log(counter1.value()); // 2
console.log(counter2.value()); // 2 (expected 0)
counter1.decrement();
console.log(counter1.value()); // 1
console.log(counter2.value()); // 1 (expected 0)
```

As we can see, the preceding example doesn't work as expected because both instances of `Counter` share the internal counter. We will learn how to fix this problem in the following section.

Private members powered by closures

In the previous section, we learned that closures can access variables that persist beyond the lexical scope from which they were created. These variables are not part of the function's prototype or body, but they are part of the function's context.

Because there is no way we can directly invoke the function's context, context variables and methods can be used to emulate private members. The main advantage of using closures to emulate private members (instead of the TypeScript private access modifier) is that closures will prevent access to private members at runtime.

TypeScript avoids emulating private properties at runtime because the compiler will throw an error at compilation time if we attempt to access a private member. TypeScript avoids using closures to emulate private members so as to improve application performance. If we add or remove an access modifier to or from one of our classes, the resulting JavaScript code will not change at all. This means that private members of a class become public members at runtime.

However, it is possible to use closures to emulate private properties at runtime. Let's look at an example:

```typescript
function makeCounter() {

    // closure context
    let _COUNTER = 0;

    function changeBy(val: number) {
        _COUNTER += val;
    }

    class Counter {

        public increment() {
            changeBy(1);
        }

        public decrement() {
            changeBy(-1);
        }

        public value() {
            return _COUNTER;
        }

    }

    return new Counter();

}
```

Please note that the preceding example is meant to be a TypeScript example.

The preceding class is almost identical to the class that we previously declared in order to demonstrate how to emulate static variables at runtime using closures.

This time, a new closure context is created every time we invoke the makeCounter function, so each new instance of Counter will remember an independent context (_COUNTER and changeBy):

```
let counter1 = makeCounter();
let counter2 = makeCounter();
console.log(counter1.value()); // 0
console.log(counter2.value()); // 0
counter1.increment();
counter1.increment();
console.log(counter1.value()); // 2
console.log(counter2.value()); // 0 (expected 0)
counter1.decrement();
console.log(counter1.value()); // 1
console.log(counter2.value()); // 0 (expected 0)
```

Since the context cannot be accessed directly, we can say that the _COUNTER variable and the changeBy function are private members even at runtime:

```
console.log(counter1.counter); // Error
console.log(counter1.changeBy(2)); // Error
```

Summary

In this chapter, we have acquired a better understanding of the runtime, which allows us to not only resolve runtime issues easily, but also to write better TypeScript code. An in-depth understanding of closures and prototypes will allow us to understand the implementation of some functional programming techniques in upcoming chapters.

In the next chapter, we will learn how to implement a number of fundamental functional programming techniques.

6
Functional Programming Techniques

After learning how to work with functions in detail, mastering asynchronous programming, and going through the main characteristics of the JavaScript runtime, we are now fully ready to focus on functional programming. In this chapter, we are going to focus on the most fundamental functional programming techniques and patterns.

We are going to try to avoid using external libraries and we are going to implement some of these techniques and patterns from scratch. This will be slightly more tedious, but it will help us to fully understand how these techniques work internally. Please note that some of these implementations have been simplified and do not cover all the potential edge cases. In an actual production system, using a well-tested functional programming library is recommended.

In this chapter, we are going to learn about the following functional programming techniques and patterns:

- Composition
- Partial application
- Currying
- Pipes
- Point-free style
- Recursion
- Pattern matching

Composition techniques

In this section, we are going to learn about some functional programming techniques that are very closely linked to function composition. We are going to learn about composition, partial application, currying, and pipes.

Composition

Functional composition is a technique or pattern that allows us to combine multiple functions to create a more complex function.

The following code snippet declares two simple functions:

```
const trim = (s: string) => s.trim();
const capitalize = (s: string) => s.toUpperCase();
```

That two simple functions declared by the preceding code snippet are the following:

- A function used to trim a string
- A function used to transform a piece of text into uppercase

We can create a function that performs both of the preceding operations by composing them as follows:

```
const trimAndCapitalize = (s: string) => capitalize(trim(s));
```

trimAndCapitalize is a function that invokes the trim function (using s as its argument) and passes its return to the capitalize function. We can invoke the trimAndCapitalize function as follows:

```
trimAndCapitalize("   hello world   "); // "HELLO WORLD"
```

The composition of two functions, f(x) and g(x), is defined as f(g(x)), and that is exactly what we have done in the implementation of the trimAndCapitalize function. However, such a behavior can be abstracted using a higher-order function:

```
const compose = <T>(f: (x: T) => T, g: (x: T) => T) => (x: T) => f(g(x));
```

We can then use the preceding function to compose two given functions:

```
const trimAndCapitalize = compose(trim, capitalize);
```

We can then invoke the trimAndCapitalize function as follows:

```
trimAndCapitalize("   hello world   "); // "HELLO WORLD"
```

One important thing to note is that the return of the g function is passed as the argument of the f function. This means that f can only take one argument (it must be a unary function). The type of the only argument of f must match the return type of the g function. These limitations can be expressed in a more correct definition of the compose function:

```
const compose = <T1, T2, T3>( f: (x: T2) => T3, g: (x: T1) => T2) => (x: T1) => f(g(x));
```

We can also compose in functions generated with the compose function:

```
const composed1 = compose(func1, func2);
const composed2 = compose(func1, func2);
const composed3 = compose(composed1, composed2);
```

Please note that the entire example is included in the companion source code.

Or we can declare a higher-order function to compose three functions in a single call:

```
const compose3 = <T1, T2, T3, T4>(
     f: (x: T3) => T4,
     g: (x: T2) => T3,
     h: (x: T1) => T2
) => (x: T1) => f(g(h(x)));
```

We can then invoke it as follows:

```
const composed1 = composeMany(func1, func2, func3);
```

We can also create a helper that allows us to compose an unlimited number of functions:

```
const composeMany = <T>(...functions: Array<(arg: T) => T>) =>
     (arg: any) =>
         functions.reduce((prev, curr) => {
             return curr(prev);
         }, arg);
```

We can then invoke it as follows:

```
const composed1 = composeMany(func1, func2, func3, func4);
const composed2 = composeMany(func1, func2, func3, func4, func5);
```

Functional composition is an extremely powerful technique, but it can be hard to put into practice in certain scenarios, for example, when our functions are not unary functions. However, there are other techniques, such as functional partial application, that can help in those scenarios, as we will see in the following section.

Partial application

Partial application is a functional programming technique that allows us to pass the arguments required by a function at different points in time.

This technique can feel like a weird idea at first glance, because most software engineers are used to the idea of applying or invoking a function at a unique point in time (complete application), as opposed to applying a function at multiple points in time (partial application).

The following code snippet implements a function that doesn't support partial application and invokes it (providing all the required arguments) at a single point in time:

```
function add(a: number, b: number) {
    return a + b;
}

const result = add(5, 5); // All arguments are provided at the same time
console.log(result); // 10
```

The following code snippet implements the preceding function using a higher-order function to allow us to provide the required arguments at different points in time:

```
function add(a: number) {
  return (b: number) => {
  return a + b;
  };
}

const add5 = add(5); // The 1st argument is provided
const result = add5(5); // The 2nd argument is provided later
console.log(result); // 10
```

As we can see in the preceding code snippet, the first and second arguments are provided at a different point in time. However, the preceding cannot be considered an example of functional partial application because the two functions are unary functions and we have provided one argument at a time.

We can also write a function that allows both its complete and partial application:

```
function add(a: number, b?: number) {
    if (b !== undefined) {
        return a + b;
    } else {
        return (b2: number) => {
            return a + b2;
        };
    }
}

const result1 = add(5, 5); // All arguments are
console.log(result1); // 10
const add5 = add(5) as (b: number) => number; // The 1st passed
const result2 = add5(5); // The 2nd argument is passed later
console.log(result2); // 10
```

The preceding example can be considered an example of partial application because we can apply a function with all its arguments (complete application), or just some of them (partial application).

Now that we know how functional partial application works, let's focus on why it is useful. In the preceding section on function composition, we learned how to compose two functions, named `trim` and `capitalize`, into a third function, named `trimAndCapitalize`:

```
const trim = (s: string) => s.trim();
const capitalize = (s: string) => s.toUpperCase();
const trimAndCapitalize = compose(trim, capitalize);
```

Function composition works very well with unary functions, but not so well with binary, ternary, or variadic functions. We are going to declare the following function to demonstrate it:

```
const replace = (s: string, f: string, r: string) => s.split(f).join(r);
```

The preceding function can be used to replace a substring in a given string. Unfortunately, the function cannot be easily used with the `compose` function because it is not a unary function:

```
const trimCapitalizeAndReplace = compose(trimAndCapitalize, replace); //
Error
```

However, we can implement the function in a way that allows us to apply the function partially:

```
const replace = (f: string, r: string) => (s: string) =>
s.split(f).join(r);
```

We can then use the `compose` function without any difficulties:

```
const trimCapitalizeAndReplace = compose(trimAndCapitalize, replace("/", "-
"));
trimCapitalizeAndReplace(" 13/feb/1989 "); // "13-FEB-1989"
```

Thanks to our knowledge of functional partial application, we can easily use the `compose` function without having to worry about the arity of the functions. However, enabling partial application requires a significant amount of manual boilerplate. In the next section, we will learn how a functional programming technique, known as **currying**, can help us to solve this problem.

Currying

Currying is a functional programming technique that allows us to partially apply a function without having to worry about the way in which we implement our functions. Currying is the process of taking a function that takes multiple arguments and transforming it into a chain of unary functions. The following function allows us to transform a function, `fn`, which takes two arguments, a and b, into a function that takes one argument, a, and returns another function that takes one argument, b:

```
function curry2<T1, T2, T3>(fn: (a: T1, b: T2) => T3) {
  return (a: T1) => (b: T2) => fn(a, b);
}
```

The above function is a higher-order function that allows our functions to be partially applied while keeping their implementation agnostic of this concern.

```
function add(a: number, b: number) {
  return a + b;
}

const curriedAdd = curry2(add);
const add5 = curriedAdd(5);
const addResult = add5(5);
console.log(addResult); // 10
```

The curry2 function allows us to transform a binary function into two unary functions. The curry2 function is a higher-order function and can be used with any binary function. For example, in the preceding code snippet, we passed the add function to the curry2 function, but the following example passes the multiply function to the curry2 function instead:

```
function multiply(a: number, b: number) {
  return a * b;
}

const curriedMultiply = curry2(multiply);
const multiplyBy5 = curriedMultiply(5);
const multiplyResult = multiplyBy5(5);
console.log(multiplyResult); // 25
```

In the preceding section on functional partial application, we learned how to use partial application to use compose with functions that are not unary. We declared the following function named replace and then passed it to the compose function:

```
const replace = (f: string, r: string) => (s: string) =>
s.split(f).join(r);

const trimCapitalizeAndReplace = compose(
    trimAndCapitalize,
    replace("/", "-")
);
```

We can declare a function named curry3, which transforms a ternary function into a chain of three unary functions:

```
function curry3<T1, T2, T3, T4>(fn: (a: T1, b: T2, c: T3) => T4) {
    return (a: T1) => (b: T2) => (c: T3) => fn(a, b, c);
}
```

We can then use the curry3 function to rewrite the replace function in a way that is agnostic of the functional partial application implementation details:

```
const replace = (s: string, f: string, r: string) => s.split(f).join(r);

const curriedReplace = curry3(replace);

const trimCapitalizeAndReplace = compose(
    trimAndCapitalize,
    curriedReplace("/")("-")
);
```

Please note that the entire example is included in the companion source code.

strictBindCallApply

We explored a few potential ways to implement partial application earlier in this chapter. However, we avoided an alternative implementation that uses the function.prototype.bind method. We have done this because the bind method was unsafe in TypeScript versions prior to the 3.2 release. If we install TypeScript version 3.2 or higher, and we enable the strictBindCallApply compilation flag in the tsconfig.json file, we will be able to use bind as follows:

```
const replace = (s: string, f: string, r: string) => s.split(f).join(r);
const replaceForwardSlash = replace.bind(replace, "/");
const replaceForwardSlashWithDash =
replaceForwardSlash.bind(replaceForwardSlash, "-");
replaceForwardSlashWithDash("13/feb/1989");
```

As we can see, the bind method allows us to apply the function partially. We can rewrite the currying example that we implemented earlier in this chapter and use the bind method instead of the currying function:

```
const compose = <T1, T2, T3>( f: (x: T2) => T3, g: (x: T1) => T2) => (x:
T1) => f(g(x));
const trim = (s: string) => s.trim();
const capitalize = (s: string) => s.toUpperCase();
const trimAndCapitalize = compose(trim, capitalize);
const replace = (s: string, f: string, r: string) => s.split(f).join(r);
const replaceForwardSlashWithDash = replace.bind(replace, "/", "-");
const trimCapitalizeAndReplace = compose(trimAndCapitalize,
replaceForwardSlashWithDash);
const result = trimCapitalizeAndReplace(" 13/feb/1989 ");
console.log(result); // "13-FEB-1989"
```

The strictBindCallApply compilation flag ensures that the return as a result of invoking the bind method will have the correct type. In versions of TypeScript prior to 3.2, the return of the bind method was of the any type.

Pipes

A `pipe` is a function or operator that allows us to pass the output of a function as the input of another. JavaScript and TypeScript don't support pipes natively (as an operator), but we can implement our pipes using the following function:

```
const pipe = <T>(...fns: Array<(arg: T) => T>) =>
    (value: T) =>
        fns.reduce((acc, fn) => fn(acc), value);
```

We are going to use the `curry3`, `trim`, `capitalize`, and `replace` functions that we declared previously in this chapter:

```
const trim = (s: string) => s.trim();
const capitalize = (s: string) => s.toUpperCase();

const replace = curry3(
  (s: string, f: string, r: string) => s.split(f).join(r)
);
```

We can then use the `pipe` function to declare a new function:

```
const trimCapitalizeAndReplace = pipe(
    trim,
    capitalize,
    replace("/")("-")
);

trimCapitalizeAndReplace(" 13/feb/1989 "); // "13-FEB-1989"
```

The `pipe` function ensures that the output of the `trim` function is passed to the `capitalize` function. The return of the `capitalize` function is then passed to the `replace` function, which has already been applied in part.

There is an official proposal to add a new operator to JavaScript known as the pipeline operator (`|>`). This operator will allow us to use pipes natively as follows:

```
const result = " 13/feb/1989 "
    |> trim
    |> capitalize
    |> replace("/")("-");
```

Please refer to the pipeline operator proposal (`https://github.com/tc39/proposal-pipeline-operator`) to learn more.

Please note that the entire example is included in the companion source code.

Other techniques

In this section, we are going to take a look at other functional programming techniques that are not directly related to function composition.

Point-free style

Point-free style, also known as **Tacit** programming, is a programming style in which function declarations do not declare the arguments (or *points*) on which they operate.

The following code snippet declares a few functions that are used to determine whether a person is eligible to vote in elections:

```
interface Person {
 age: number;
 birthCountry: string;
 naturalizationDate: Date;
}

const OUR_COUNTRY = "Ireland";
const wasBornInCountry = (person: Person) => person.birthCountry ===
OUR_COUNTRY;
const wasNaturalized = (person: Person) =>
Boolean(person.naturalizationDate);
const isOver18 = (person: Person) => person.age >= 18;
const isCitizen = (person: Person) => wasBornInCountry(person) ||
wasNaturalized(person);
const isEligibleToVote = (person: Person) => isOver18(person) &&
isCitizen(person);

isEligibleToVote({
    age: 27,
    birthCountry: "Ireland",
    naturalizationDate: new Date(),
});
```

The preceding code snippet didn't use any of the functional programming techniques that we have already learned in this chapter. The following code snippet implements an alternative solution for the same problem using techniques such as partial application. This code snippet declares two functions, named `both` and `either`, that can be used to determine whether a variable matches the requirements specified by some or both functions provided to these functions:

 The `either` and `both` functions are simplified implementations of some real algebraic data types. We will learn more about algebraic data types and category theory in the next chapter.

```
const either = <T1>(
  funcA: (a: T1) => boolean,
  funcB: (a: T1) => boolean
) => (arg: T1) => funcA(arg) || funcB(arg);

const both = <T1>(
  funcA: (a: T1) => boolean,
  funcB: (a: T1) => boolean
) => (arg: T1) => funcA(arg) && funcB(arg);


interface Person {
  age: number;
  birthCountry: string;
  naturalizationDate: Date;
}

const OUR_COUNTRY = "Ireland";
const wasBornInCountry = (person: Person) => person.birthCountry ===
OUR_COUNTRY;
const wasNaturalized = (person: Person) =>
Boolean(person.naturalizationDate);
const isOver18 = (person: Person) => person.age >= 18;

// Point-free style

const isCitizen = either(wasBornInCountry, wasNaturalized);
const isEligibleToVote = both(isOver18, isCitizen);

isEligibleToVote({
  age: 27,
  birthCountry: "Ireland",
  naturalizationDate: new Date(),
});
```

As we can see, the `isCitizen` and `isElegibleToVote` functions take some functions as arguments, but they don't mention which data types they expect as arguments. For example, instead of writing the following:

```
const isCitizen = (person: Person) => wasBornInCountry(person) ||
wasNaturalized(person);
```

We can write the following:

```
const isCitizen = either(wasBornInCountry, wasNaturalized);
```

This style, in which we avoid referencing function arguments, is known as the point-free style, and it has a number of advantages over the more conventional function declaration style:

- It makes programs simpler and more concise. This isn't always a good thing, but it can be.
- It makes algorithms easier to understand by focusing only on the functions being combined. We get a better sense of what's going on without the data arguments getting in the way.
- It forces us to think more about how data is used than about which data is being used.
- It helps us think about our functions as generic building blocks that can work with different kinds of data, rather than thinking about them as operations on one kind of data.

 Please note that the entire example is included in the companion source code.

Recursion

A function that calls itself is known as a recursive function. The following function is a recursive function and allows us to calculate the factorial of a given number, n. The factorial is the product of all positive integers less than, or equal to, a given number, n:

```
const factorial = (n: number): number => (n === 0) ? 1 : (n * factorial(n -
1));
```

We can invoke the preceding function as follows:

```
factorial(5); // 120
```

In general, you should try to implement functions without recursion. Using recursion should be considered carefully because the JavaScript runtime is not very efficient at handling it since, in a recursive function call, a frame is added to the stack with each function call.

Pattern matching

Pattern matching allows you to match a value (or an object) against some patterns to select a branch of the code. In functional languages, pattern matching can be used to match on standard primitive values such as strings. TypeScript allows us to implement pattern matching using literal types and control flow analysis.

For example, we can define three types, named `Circle`, `Square`, and `Rectangle`. We can then define a new type, named `Shape`, which is the union of the `Circle`, `Square`, and `Rectangle` types:

```
const enum ShapeKind {
    circle = "circle",
    square = "square",
    rectangle = "rectangle",
}

type Circle = { kind: ShapeKind.circle, radius: number };
type Square = { kind: ShapeKind.square, size: number };
type Rectangle = { kind: ShapeKind.rectangle, w: number, h: number };
type Shape = Circle | Square | Rectangle;
```

We can then implement functions that take an argument of the `Shape` type and use pattern matching to identify whether the `Shape` is a `Circle`, a `Square`, or a `Rectangle`:

```
function area(shape: Shape) {
    switch(shape.kind) {
        case ShapeKind.circle:
            return shape.radius ** 2;
        case ShapeKind.square:
            return shape.size ** 2;
        case ShapeKind.rectangle:
            return shape.w * shape.h;
        default:
            throw new Error("Invalid shape!");
    }
}
```

Pattern matching was impossible in versions of TypeScript prior to 2.0 because control flow analysis and literal types were not available.

Summary

In this chapter, we have learned some of the main functional programming techniques and patterns, including functional composition, functional partial application, and currying.

In the next chapter, we are going to learn about category theory. We will learn how to work with some algebraic data types and how they can help make our TypeScript applications more robust.

7
Category Theory

In the previous chapter, we learned about functions, asynchronous programming, and the runtime and functional programming principles and techniques, including pure functions and functional composition.

In this chapter, we are going to focus on category theory and algebraic data types. We are going to learn about the following concepts:

- Category theory
- Algebraic data types
- Functors
- Applicative
- Maybe
- Either
- Monads

Category theory

Functional programming has a reputation for being difficult to learn and understand due to its mathematical background. Functional programming languages and design patterns are influenced by concepts that originated in different mathematical fields. However, we can highlight **category theory** as one of the most significant influences. We can think about category theory as an alternative to set theory. It defines the theory behind a series of data structures or objects known as **algebraic data types**.

There are many algebraic data types, and understanding all the properties and rules that they must implement requires a significant amount of time and effort. The following diagram illustrates the relationships between some of the most common algebraic data types:

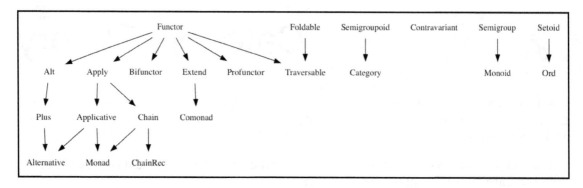

The arrows in the diagram indicate that a given algebraic data type must implement the specification of some other algebraic data types. For example, the **Monad** type must implement the specifications of the **Applicative** and **Chain** types.

The open source project, fantasy-land, declares a specification for some of these algebraic data types. The open source project, ramda-fantasy, implements these specifications in a way that is compatible with Ramda, which is a popular functional programming library that we will explore later in this book.

The algebraic data type specifications can be implemented in many ways. For example, the `Functor` specification can be implemented by a `Maybe` or an `Either` data type. Both types implement the `Functor` specification, but can also implement other specifications, such as the `Monad` or the `Applicative` specification.

The following table describes which specifications (listed in the top row) are implemented by one of the algebraic data type implementations (left row) in the fantasy-ramda project:

Name	Setoid	Semigroup	Functor	Applicative	Monad	Foldable	ChainRec
Either	✔	✘	✔	✔	✔	✘	✔
Future	✘	✘	✔	✔	✔	✘	✔
Identity	✔	✘	✔	✔	✔	✘	✔
IO	✘	✘	✔	✔	✔	✘	✔
Maybe	✔	✔	✔	✔	✔	✔	✔
Reader	✘	✘	✔	✔	✔	✘	✘
Tuple	✔	✔	✔	✘	✘	✘	✘
State	✘	✘	✔	✔	✔	✘	✔

Understanding the field of category theory and all these data types and specifications is outside the scope of this book. However, in this chapter, we are going to learn the basics regarding two of the most common algebraic data types: Functors and Monads.

 Please refer to the fantasy-land project at https://github.com/fantasyland/fantasy-land and the fantasy-ramda project at https://github.com/ramda/ramda-fantasy to learn more about algebraic data types.

Functors

The Functor type has two main characteristics:

- It holds a value
- It implements a method named map

The following code snippet declares a class named Container. This class can be considered a Functor:

```
class Container<T> {

    private _value: T;

    public constructor(val: T) {
        this._value = val;
    }

    public map<TMap>(fn: (val: T) => TMap) {
        return new Container<TMap>(fn(this._value));
    }

}
```

We can use the container as follows:

```
const double = (x: number) => x + x;
const container = new Container(3);
const container2 = container.map(double);
console.log(container2); // { _value: 6 }
```

At this point, you may think that the `Functor` type is not very useful because we have implemented the most basic version possible. The next two sections implement two `Functors` known as `Maybe` and `Either`. These two `Functors` are much more useful and will demonstrate that `Functors` are a powerful tool. However, before we can implement the `Maybe` and `Either` types, we need to learn about the `Applicative` type.

Applicative

An `Applicative` is a `Functor` that implements a method named `of`. However, an `Applicative` is not just a `Functor` type; it is also an `Apply` type. For a type to be an implementation of `Apply`, it must implement a method named `ap` that takes a `Functor` that wraps a function as an argument.

The following code snippet implements an `Applicative` and, as a result, it has an `of`, a `map`, and an `ap` method:

```
class Container<T> {

    public static of<TVal>(val: TVal) {
        return new Container(val);
    }

    private _value!: T;

    public constructor(val: T) {
        this._value = val;
    }

    public map<TMap>(fn: (val: T) => TMap) {
        return new Container<TMap>(fn(this._value));
    }

    public ap<TMap>(c: Container<(val: T) => TMap>) {
        return c.map(fn => this.map(fn));
    }

}
```

We can use the `Applicative` to wrap a number and a function as follows:

```
const double = (x: number) => x + x;
const numberContainer = Container.of(3);
const functionContainer = Container.of(double);
```

We can use the `map` method to map the value wrapped by the `Functor` using a mapping function:

```
numberContainer.map(double); // Returns Container<number> with value 6
```

Alternatively, we can use the `ap` function to perform the same operation using a `Functor` that wraps a function instead of a function:

```
numberContainer.ap(functionContainer); // Container<number> with value 6
```

 Please note that the entire example is included in the companion source code.

Maybe

The following `Maybe` data type is a `Functor` and an `Applicative`, which means that it contains a value and implements the `map` method. The main difference with the preceding implementation of `Functor` is that the value contained is optional:

```
class MayBe<T> {

    public static of<TVal>(val?: TVal) {
        return new MayBe(val);
    }

    private _value!: T;

    public constructor(val?: T) {
        if (val) {
            this._value = val;
        }
    }

    public isNothing() {
        return (this._value === null || this._value === undefined);
    }
```

```
    public map<TMap>(fn: (val: T) => TMap) {
        if (this.isNothing()) {
            return new MayBe<TMap>();
        } else {
            return new MayBe<TMap>(fn(this._value));
        }
    }

    public ap<TMap>(c: MayBe<(val: T) => TMap>) {
        return c.map(fn => this.map(fn));
    }

}
```

As we can see in the preceding implementation of the map method, the mapping function is only applied if the Maybe data type contains a value.

To demonstrate how to use the Maybe type and why it is useful, we are going to declare a function to fetch the latest TypeScript news from www.reddit.com, as follows:

```
interface New {
    subreddit: string;
    id: string;
    title: string;
    score: number;
    over_18: boolean;
    url: string;
    author: string;
    ups: number;
    num_comments: number;
    created_utc: number;
}

interface Response {
    kind: string;
    data: {
        modhash: string;
        whitelist_status: boolean|null;
        children: Array<{ kind: string, data: New }>;
        after: string|null;
        before: string|null;
    };
}

async function fetchNews() {
    return new Promise<MayBe<Response>>((resolve, reject) => {
        const url = "https://www.reddit.com/r/typescript/new.json";
        fetch(url)
```

```
            .then((response) => {
                return response.json();
            }).then((json) => {
                resolve(new MayBe(json));
            }).catch(() => {
                resolve(new MayBe());
            });
        });
    }
```

The preceding code snippet uses the fetch API to send an HTTP request. This is an asynchronous operation, which explains why the snippet creates a Promise instance. When the operations are completed successfully, the response is returned as a Maybe instance that contains a value. When the operations are completed unsuccessfully, an empty Maybe instance is returned.

The following code snippet demonstrates how we can use the fetchNews function:

```
(async () => {

    const maybeOfResponse = await fetchNews();

    const maybeOfNews = maybeOfResponse
        .map(r => r.data)
        .map(d => d.children)
        .map(children => children.map(c => c.data));

    maybeOfNews.map((news) => {
        news.forEach((n) => console.log(`${n.title} - ${n.url}`));
        return news;
    });

})();
```

The preceding code snippet uses the fetchNews function to fetch a list of posts concerning TypeScript from Reddit. If the request is completed successfully, the fetchNews function returns the HTTP response wrapped in a MayBe instance. We then use the map method to find the list of posts within the response. The nice thing about using a MayBe instance is that mapping logic is only executed if there is an actual response, so we don't need to worry about potential null or undefined errors.

Please note that the preceding example uses some browser APIs, which means that we need to add dom to the lib field in our tsconfig.json file. We are also using the async keyword, which requires the es6 in lib. This will prevent compilation errors such as **Cannot find name fetch**.

Please note that the entire example is included in the companion source code.

Either

The Either algebraic data type is the union of the Just and Nothing types:

```
type Either<T1, T2> = Just<T1> | Nothing<T2>;
```

The just type is a Functor used to represent a non-nullable value:

```
class Nothing<T> {

    public static of<TVal>(val?: TVal) {
        return new Nothing(val);
    }

    private _value: T|undefined;

    public constructor(val?: T) {
        this._value = val;
    }

    public map<TMap>(fn: (val: T) => TMap) {
        if (this._value !== undefined) {
            return new Nothing<TMap>(fn(this._value));
        } else {
            return new Nothing<TMap>(this._value as any);
        }
    }

}
```

The Nothing type represents the lack of a value:

```
class Just<T> {

    public static of<TVal>(val: TVal) {
        return new Just(val);
    }

    private _value: T;

    public constructor(val: T) {
        this._value = val;
    }

    public map<TMap>(fn: (val: T) => TMap) {
        return new Just<TMap>(fn(this._value));
    }

}
```

The following code snippet is an implementation of the fetchNews function that we declared in the preceding section. The main difference this time is that we will return an instance of Just if the HTTP request is completed successfully, and an instance of Nothing if the HTTP request is not completed successfully:

```
interface New {
    subreddit: string;
    id: string;
    title: string;
    score: number;
    over_18: boolean;
    url: string;
    author: string;
    ups: number;
    num_comments: number;
    created_utc: number;
}

interface Response {
    kind: string;
    data: {
        modhash: string;
        whitelist_status: boolean|null;
        children: Array<{ kind: string, data: New }>;
        after: string|null;
        before: string|null;
    };
}
```

```
async function fetchNews() {
    return new Promise<Either<Response, Error>>((resolve, reject) => {

        const url = "https://www.reddit.com/r/typescript/new.json";

        fetch(url)
            .then((response) => {
                return response.json();
            }).then((json) => {
                resolve(new Just(json));
            }).catch((e) => {
                resolve(new Nothing(e));
            });

    });
}
```

If we try to use map on an Either instance, we will get a compilation error:

```
(async () => {

    const maybeOfResponse = await fetchNews();

    maybeOfResponse.map(r => r.message);
    // Error:
    // Cannot invoke an expression whose type lacks a call signature.
    // Type
    // (<TMap>(fn: (val: Response) => TMap) => Just<TMap>) |
    // (<TMap>(fn: (val: Error) => TMap) => Nothin<TMap>'
    // has no compatible call signatures.

})();
```

We can use a type guard to ensure that we are accessing a Nothing instance when a request fails, and a Just instance when a request is completed without errors:

```
(async () => {

    const maybeOfResponse = await fetchNews();

    if (maybeOfResponse instanceof Nothing) {

        maybeOfResponse
            .map(r => r.message)
            .map(msg => {
                console.log(`Error: ${msg}`);
                return msg;
            });
```

```
        } else {

            const maybeOfNews = maybeOfResponse.map(r => r.data)
                .map(d => d.children)
                .map(children => children.map(c => c.data));

            maybeOfNews.map((news) => {
                news.forEach((n) => console.log(`${n.title} - ${n.url}`));
                return news;
            });

        }

})();
```

The good thing about using `Either` is that the compiler forces us to use a type guard. This means that using `Either` can lead to increased type safety when dealing with potential failures in I/O operations such as HTTP requests.

 Please note that the entire example is included in the companion source code.

Monads

We are going to finish our introduction to algebraic data types by learning about monads. A `Monad` is a `Functor`, but it also implements the `Applicative` and `Chain` specifications.

We can transform the previously declared `Maybe` data type into a `Monad` by adding two extra methods named `join` and `chain`:

```
class MayBe<T> {

    public static of<TVal>(val?: TVal) {
        return new MayBe(val);
    }

    private _value!: T;

    public constructor(val?: T) {
        if (val) {
            this._value = val;
        }
    }
```

```
    public isNothing() {
        return (this._value === null || this._value === undefined);
    }

    public map<TMap>(fn: (val: T) => TMap) {
        if (this.isNothing()) {
            return new MayBe<TMap>();
        } else {
            return new MayBe<TMap>(fn(this._value));
        }
    }

    public ap<TMap>(c: MayBe<(val: T) => TMap>) {
        return c.map(fn => this.map(fn));
    }

    public join() {
        return this.isNothing() ? Nothing.of(this._value) : this._value;
    }

    public chain<TMap>(fn: (val: T) => TMap) {
        return this.map(fn).join();
    }

}
```

The `Maybe` data type was already a `Functor` and an `Applicative`, but now it is also a `Monad`. The following code snippet showcases how we can use it:

```
let maybeOfNumber = MayBe.of(5);
maybeOfNumber.map((a) => a * 2);
// MayBe { value: 10 }

maybeOfNumber.join();
// 5

maybeOfNumber.chain((a) => a * 2);
// 10

let maybeOfMaybeOfNumber = MayBe.of(MayBe.of(5));
// MayBe { value: MayBe { value: 5 } }

maybeOfMaybeOfNumber.map((a) => a.map(v => v * 2));
// MayBe { value: MayBe { value: 10 } }

maybeOfMaybeOfNumber.join();
// MayBe { value: 5 }
```

```
maybeOfMaybeOfNumber.chain((a) => a.map(v => v * 2));
// MayBe { value: 10 }
```

The preceding code snippet demonstrates how the `join` and `chain` methods work. As you can see, they are very useful when we have a `Functor` of a `Functor`, and we want to access the contained value. The `chain` method is just a one-step shortcut for the two operations, `join` and `map`.

 Please note that the entire example is included in the companion source code.

Summary

In this chapter, we have learned about a number of algebraic data types, including the `Functor`, `Nothing`, `Just`, `Maybe`, `Either`, and `Monad` data types. We have learned how these types can help us to ensure that certain errors are handled correctly by our code.

In the next chapter, we are going to learn about other functional programming constructs known as Optics, as well as two new powerful techniques: lazy evaluation and immutability.

Immutability, Optics, and Laziness

8

In the preceding chapters, we learned the most fundamental functional programming techniques and patterns, including some of the most commonly known algebraic data types.

In this chapter, we are going to learn about a number of additional functional programming techniques and patterns, including the following:

- Immutability
- Optics
- Lenses
- Prims
- Lazy evaluation

Once more, we will try to build everything from scratch, trying to avoid the use of third-party libraries. Our goal is to take a look at the internal implementation of some of these techniques and patterns so we can fully understand how they work. Let's get started!

Immutability

In this section, we are going to learn about immutable data structures. An immutable data structure is an object that doesn't allow us to change its value. The easiest way to implement an immutable data structure in TypeScript is to use classes and the `readonly` keyword:

```
class Person {

    public readonly name: string;
    public readonly age: number;
```

```
    public constructor(name: string, age: number) {
        this.name = name;
        this.age = age;
    }

}

const person = new Person("Remo", 29);
person.age = 30; // Error
person.name = "Remo Jansen"; // Error
```

The preceding code snippet declares a class named Person. The class has two public properties, named name and age. These two properties have been flagged as readonly. As we can see in the code snippet, when we try to update the values of the class properties, a compilation error is thrown.

The readonly properties can make our code more secure because it protects us from state mutations. For example, if we pass some immutable objects to a function as its arguments, the function will not be able to mutate the original objects. This means that our function will be more likely to be a pure function. However, not everything is good about immutable objects. Working with immutable objects can sometimes feel very tedious and verbose, particularly when we wish to generate a new state. Let's take a look at an example:

```
class Street {

    public readonly num: number;
    public readonly name: string;

    public constructor(num: number, name: string) {
        this.num = num;
        this.name = name;
    }

}

class Address {

    public readonly city: string;
    public readonly street: Street;

    public constructor(city: string, street: Street) {
        this.city = city;
        this.street = street;
    }

}
```

```
class Company {

    public readonly name: string;
    public readonly addresses: Address[];

    public constructor(name: string, addresses: Address[]) {
        this.name = name;
        this.addresses = addresses;
    }

}
```

The preceding code snippet declares three classes named Street, Address, and Company. All the properties in the three classes are readonly, which means that the classes are immutable. We can create a new instance of the Company class as follows:

```
const company1 = new Company(
    "Facebook",
    [
        new Address(
            "London",
            new Street(1, "rathbone square")
        ),
        new Address(
            "Dublin",
            new Street(5, "grand canal square")
        )
    ]
);
```

When we say that an object is immutable, it means that we cannot change the original object, but it doesn't mean that we don't want to create derivative versions of it. For example, if we try to create a new version of a Company by transforming its street name into upper case, we will get an error, as shown in the following code snippet:

```
company1.addresses = company1.addresses.map(a => R.toUpper(a.street.name));
// Error
```

However, we might need to generate a new version with an uppercase street name. We can generate an updated version of the Company instance by creating a new Company instance. To create a new copy, we need to copy all the properties from the original instance into a new instance and use new values for the properties that we wish to mutate:

```
const company2 = new Company(
    company1.name,
    company1.addresses.map((a) =>
        new Address(
```

```
            a.city,
            new Street(
                a.street.num,
                R.toUpper(a.street.name)
            )
        )
    )
);
```

Immutable data structures can help us to implement pure functions and make our code free of side effects. Mutating external variables is one of the most common causes of side effects, and using immutable data structures can help us to prevent such a mutation.

 Please note that you can refer to `Chapter 1`, *Functional Programming Fundamentals*, to learn more about side effects.

However, as we can see in the previous code snippet, immutable data structures also have a negative side: they can lead to verbose and tedious code. The good news is that the minds behind the functional programming paradigm have found a solution to this problem known as **optics**. We are going to learn about optics in the following section.

Optics

Optics is a functional programming concept that can help us to reduce the amount of code that we need to write and make operations more readable. The benefits of using optics are particularly noticeable when we are working with immutable data structures. All optics are a way to get and set properties in an object. In fact, we can think about optics as an alternative to getters and setters in object-oriented programming.

Optics can be categorized into two main groups—**lenses** and **prisms**. As we learned in `Chapter 7`, *Category Theory*, algebraic data types can be defined in terms of sum and product types. A lens is used to work with product types (for example, tuples and objects) and a prism is used to work with sum types (for example, discriminated unions). During the remainder of this section, we are going to focus on the use of lenses.

Lenses

A lens is just a pair of functions that allow us to get and set a value in an object. The interface of a lens could be declared as follows:

```
interface Lens<T1, T2> {
    get(o: T1): T2;
    set(o: T2, v: T1): T1;
}
```

As we can see in the previous code snippet, the lens generic interface declares two methods. The `get` method can be used to get the value of a property of type `T2` in an object of type `T1`. The `set` method can be used for the value of a property with type `T2` in an object of type `T1`. The following code snippet implements the `Lens` interface:

```
const streetLens: Lens<Address, Street> = {
    get: (o: Address) => o.street,
    set: (v: Street, o: Address) => new Address(o.city, v)
};
```

The preceding implementation of the `Lens` interface is named `streetLens` and it allows us to set the value of a property with the `Street` type in an object of type `Object`. We can use the `streetLens` object to get the `Street` instance in an `Address` instance:

```
const address = new Address(
    "London",
    new Street(1, "rathbone square")
);

const street = streetLens.get(address);
```

We can also use the `Lens` implementation to set the `Street` instance in the `Address` instance:

```
const address2 = streetLens.set(
    new Street(
        address.street.num,
        R.toUpper(address.street.name)
    ),
    address
);
```

It is important to note that the `set` method updates the `Street` instance and returns a new `Address` instance, as opposed to mutating the original `Address` instance. Now that we know the basics of how lenses work, we are going to take a look at some of the properties.

One of the main characteristics of lenses is that they can be composed. As we learned in the preceding chapters, function composition is one of the main techniques in functional programming, and lenses are just functions, so they can be composed in a very similar way. The following code snippet declares a higher-order function that allows us to compose two lenses:

```
function composeLens<A, B, C>(
    ab: Lens<A, B>,
    bc: Lens<B, C>
): Lens<A, C> {
    return {
        get: (a: A) => bc.get(ab.get(a)),
        set: (c: C, a: A) => ab.set(bc.set(c, ab.get(a)), a)
    };
}
```

Now that we have declared a higher-order function that allows us to compose lenses, we are going to compose two lenses named `streetLens` and `nameLens`:

```
const streetLens: Lens<Address, Street> = {
    get: (o: Address) => o.street,
    set: (v: Street, o: Address) => new Address(o.city, v)
};

const nameLens: Lens<Street, string> = {
    get: (o: Street) => o.name,
    set: (v: string, o: Street) => new Street(o.num, v)
};

const streetNameLens = composeLens(streetLens, nameLens);
```

The return of the `composeLens` function creates a new lens named `streetName`. The new lens can be used to get the name of a `Street` instance within an `Address` instance:

```
const address = new Address(
    "London",
    new Street(1, "rathbone square")
);

const streetName = streetNameLens.get(address);
```

The lens can also be used to create a new `Address` instance with an updated `Street` name:

```
const address2 = streetNameLens.set(R.toUpper(address.street.name),
address);
```

Many functional programming libraries also implement a function that allows us to map a given property in an object to a new value using a lens. The function is sometimes named `over`, but we are going to name it `overLens` to be clearer:

```
function overLens<S, A>(
    lens: Lens<S, A>,
    func: (a: A) => A,
    s: S
): S {
    return lens.set(func(lens.get(s)), s)
}
```

The preceding function takes a lens as its first argument, a mapping function as its second argument, and an object as its third argument. The function uses the lens to focus and update one of the properties of the objects using the mapping function:

```
const address = new Address(
    "London",
    new Street(1, "rathbone square")
);

const address2 = overLens(streetNameLens, R.toUpper, address);
```

As you can see, generating new versions of immutable objects using lenses can be much less verbose and tedious than using standard property accessors and class constructors. Now that we know the basics about lenses, we are going to implement some lenses again. The previous implementation was simplified to facilitate understanding. This time however, we are going to implement lenses in a way that is closer to the implementation of some popular libraries such as Ramda.

This time, we are going to declare two functions that are used as a getter and a setter. The function that is used as a getter is going to implement an interface named `Prop`. On the other hand, the function used as a setter is going to implement an interface named `Assoc`. The signature of the `Prop` and `Assoc` interfaces appears as follows:

```
type Prop<T, K extends keyof T> = (o: T) => T[K];
type Assoc<T, K extends keyof T> = (v: T[K], o: T) => T;
```

The following code snippet declares functions that
implement the Prop and Assoc interfaces. Both implementations are used to access a
property named street in an object of type Address:

```
const propStreet: Prop<Address, "street"> = (o: Address) => o.street;

const assocStreet: Assoc<Address, "street"> = (v: Address["street"], o:
Address) => {
    return new Address(o.city, v);
};
```

One of the main differences in the new implementation is that we are going to declare a
higher-order function named lens, and we are going to use it to generate a lens instance.
The lens function takes two functions, a getter and a setter, which implement the Prop
and Assoc interfaces accordingly. The lens function then returns an implementation of the
Lens interface:

```
const lens = <T1, K extends keyof T1>(
    getter: Prop<T1, K>,
    setter: Assoc<T1, K>,
): Lens<T1, T1[K]> => {
    return {
        get: (obj: T1) => getter(obj),
        set: (val: T1[K], obj: T1) => setter(val, obj),
    };
}
```

At this point, we can invoke the lens function using the getter function, propStreet, and
the setter function, assocStreet, that we declared previously:

```
const streetLens = lens(propStreet, assocStreet);
```

Another significant difference is that the new implementation uses two more functions,
named view and set, as the getter and setter respectively. Both the view and set functions
take a lens instance:

```
const view = <T1, T2>(lens: Lens<T1, T2>, obj: T1) => lens.get(obj);

const set = <T1, K extends keyof T1>(
    lens: Lens<T1, T1[K]>,
    val: T1[K],
    obj: T1
) => lens.set(val, obj);
```

The preceding functions use the lens `get` and `set` methods internally. However, we will use the `view` and `set` functions instead. The following code snippet demonstrates how to use the `view` function to get the `Street` instance within an `Address` instance:

```
const address = new Address(
    "London",
    new Street(1, "rathbone square")
);

const street = view(streetLens, address);
```

The following code snippet demonstrates how to use the set function to set the value of the `Street` instance within an `Address` instance:

```
const address2 = set(
    streetLens,
    new Street(
        address.street.num,
        R.toUpper(address.street.name)
    ),
    address
);
```

In this section, we have learned the basics regarding lenses. In the following section, we are going to learn about another kind of functional optic, known as **prisms**.

Prisms

Prisms are almost identical to lenses. We can think about a prism as a kind of lens that allows us to get and set an optional property in an object. The most significant difference between lenses and prisms is that prisms can work with optional types.

The following code snippet declares the `Prism` interface. As we can see, the `Prism` interface is very similar to the `Lens` interface. However, the `get` method returns an optional type, `Maybe<T>`:

```
type Maybe<T> = T | null;

interface Prism<T1, T2> {
    get(o: T1): Maybe<T2>,
    set(a: T2, o: T1): T1;
}
```

Just like lenses, prisms can be composed. The following code snippet declares a higher-order function that allows us to compose two prisms:

```
function composePrism<A, B, C>(ab: Prism<A, B>, bc: Prism<B, C>): Prism<A,
C> {
    return {
        get: (a: A) => {
            const b = ab.get(a)
            return b == null ? null : bc.get(b)
        },
        set: (c: C, a: A) => {
            const b = ab.get(a)
            return b == null ? a : ab.set(bc.set(c, b), a)
        }
    }
}
```

The preceding function takes two prisms, ab with type Prism<A, B>, and bc with type Prism<B, C>, and returns the composition of both prisms with type Prism<A, C>.

Prisms also allow us to implement a function that allows us to map a property given an object and a prism. The function is usually named over in real-world libraries but, just as we did in the section about lenses, we are going to name it overPrism for clarity:

```
function overPrism<S, A>(
    prism: Prism<S, A>,
    func: (a: A) => A,
    s: S
): S {
    const a = prism.get(s)
    return a ? prism.set(func(a), s) : s
}
```

In the preceding snippet, we have declared the main building blocks required to work with prisms, including the Prism interface and the composePrism and overPrism functions. In the following section, we are going to demonstrate how to use a prism named firstCharacterPrism to focus on the first character of an optional string. The code snippet also declares a prism to access the street property in an Address instance and the name property in a Street instance.

The `composePrism` is then used to compose the three `firstCharacterPrism`, `streetPrism`, and `namePrism` prisms into a new prism named `streetNameFirstCharater`. Finally, the `overPrism` function is used to map the value selected by `streetNameFirstCharacter` using the `R.toUpper` function. The result is a new instance of `Address` that contains a new instance of `Street` with a capitalized name. If the name is `null`, the new `Street` instance will contain `null` as its name:

```
const firstCharacterPrism: Prism<string, string> = {
    get: s => s ? s.substring(0, 1) : null,
    set: (a, s) => s.length ? a + s.substring(1) : ""
}

const streetPrism: Prism<Address, Street> = {
    get: (o: Address) => o.street,
    set: (v: Street, o: Address) => new Address(o.city, v)
};

const namePrism: Prism<Street, string> = {
    get: (o: Street) => o.name,
    set: (v: string, o: Street) => new Street(o.num, v)
};

const address = new Address(
    "London",
    new Street(1, "rathbone square")
);

const streetNameFirstCharacterPrism = composePrism(
    composePrism(streetPrism, namePrism),
    firstCharacterPrism
);

const address2 = overPrism(streetNameFirstCharacterPrism, R.toUpper,
address);
```

Prisms are also useful when we want to work with other kinds of optional types, such as discriminated unions like the `Either` type:

```
type Either<T1, T2> = T1 | T2;

type Domicile = Either<
    { type: "office", address: Address },
    { type: "personal", address: string }
>;

const addressPrism: Prism<Domicile, Address> = {
    get: d => d.type === "office" ? d.address : null,
```

```
    set: (address, d) => d.type === "office" ? { type: "office", address }
  : d
  }
```

The preceding code snippet declares an optional type named `Either` and a type named `Domicile`, which uses the `Either` type to declare the union of two types. The code snippet also declares a `prism` named `addressPrism` that allows us to get or set the property `address` in an object of type `Domicile`. The property `address` can either be a `string` or an `Address` instance, and the `addressPrism` can handle both cases, as demonstrated by the following code snippet:

```
const address = new Address(
    "London",
    new Street(1, "rathbone square")
);

const domicile1: Domicile = { type: "office", address: address };
const domicile2: Domicile = { type: "personal", address: "23 high street"
};

const address1 = addressPrism.get(domicile1);
const address2 = addressPrism.get(domicile2);
```

At this point, we should understand the main characteristics of both lenses and prisms. In this chapter, we have created our own implementations of lenses and prisms because our main goal was to understand how they work. However, using a custom implementation is not recommended for professional software development projects. In `Chapter 10`, *Real-World Functional Programming*, we will learn how to use production-ready optics with Ramda.

In the following section, we are going to learn about lazy evaluation.

Laziness

Lazy evaluation is a technique or pattern that delays the evaluation of an expression until its value is needed. We are going to take a look at an example that doesn't use lazy evaluation first so that we can compare it with one that uses lazy evaluation later.

The following code snippet declares an interface named `Dog` and an array of `Dog` that contains ten items. The `Dog` instances have two properties, named `size` and `name`. The code snippet also declares two functions, named `isLarge` and `isOld`. The `isLarge` function is used to find the `Dog` instances, with their `size` being equal to `"L"`. The `isOld` function is used to find the `Dog` instances with an `age` greater than 5:

```
interface Dog {
    size: "L" | "S";
    age: number;
    name: string;
}

const dogs: Dog[] = [
    { size: "S", age: 4, name: "Alice" },
    { size: "L", age: 2, name: "Bob", },
    { size: "S", age: 7, name: "Carol" },
    { size: "L", age: 6, name: "Dan" },
    { size: "L", age: 2, name: "Eve" },
    { size: "S", age: 2, name: "Frank" },
    { size: "S", age: 1, name: "Grant" },
    { size: "S", age: 9, name: "Hans" },
    { size: "L", age: 8, name: "Inga" },
    { size: "L", age: 4, name: "Julia" }
];

const isLarge = (dog: Dog) => dog.size === "L";
const isOld = (dog: Dog) => dog.age > 5;
dogs.filter(isLarge).find(isOld); // Dan
```

The preceding code snippet uses the array methods, `filter` and `find`. The `filter` method iterates all the elements in the `dogs` array. The result of filtering all the `Dog` instances using the `isLarge` function is a new array with five elements (all the elements with a `size` equal to `"L"`). We then use the `find` method to search a `Dog` instance in the new array using the `isOld` function. The `find` method iterates two items before the first item with an `age` greater than 5 is found. The final result is that we need to iterate 12 items before we can find an item that matches both the `isLarge` and `isOld` constraints.

Lazy evaluation is a technique that delays the execution of some operations until they can no longer be delayed. Lazy evaluation can sometimes lead to performance gains.

The following code snippet implements a function named `filter` and a function named `find`. Both functions are the equivalent of the array `filter` and `find` methods respectively. However, the `filter` function uses a generator (`function*`) and the `find` function uses a `for ... of` statement, which is used to iterate the items returned by the iterator created by the preceding generator:

```
const filter = <T>(f: (item: T) => boolean) => {
    return function* (arr: T[]) {
        for (const item of arr) {
            if (f(item)) {
                yield item;
            }
        }
    };
};

const find = <T>(f: (item: T) => boolean) =>(arr: IterableIterator<T>) => {
    for (const item of arr) {
        if (f(item)) {
            return item;
        }
    }
};
```

 Please remember that using iterators requires the compilation setting `downlevelIteration` to be true in the `tsconfig.json` file. Please refer to Chapter 3, *Mastering Asynchronous Programming,* if you need additional help with generators.

The code snippet uses the `compose` function from Ramda to compose the return of `find(isOld)` and `filter(isLarge)`. The result is a new function named `findLargeOldDog`. We can use this function to find the `Dog` instances in the `dogs` array that matches both the `isLarge` and `isOld` constraints:

```
const findLargeOldDog = R.compose(find(isOld), filter(isLarge));
findLargeOldDog(dogs);
```

The result of this function is identical to the result of the example that didn't use lazy evaluation. However, this example only iterates four items instead of twelve. This is the case because when we execute the filter function, filtering doesn't take place. We delay its evaluation by returning an iterator. The evaluation is delayed until the iterator's `next` method is invoked by the `for ... of` statement. The find function iterates one item at a time and invokes both the `isOld` and `isLarge` functions, one item at a time. When the iterator returns the fourth item, it matches both the `isLarge` and `isOld` constraints and no more items need to be iterated. The lazy evaluated version is therefore much more efficient.

In the preceding example, we have used generators and iterators to implement lazy evaluation, but this is not the only way to implement lazy evaluation. Lazy evaluation can be implemented using several JavaScript APIs, such as proxies or promises.

Summary

In this chapter, we have learned how we can leverage functional programming techniques, such as lazy evaluation and immutability, to prevent some potential issues. We have also learned how to use optics to be able to work with immutable objects in a less verbose and tedious way.

In the next chapter, we are going to learn about **Functional Reactive Programming** (FRP). We will learn what reactive programming is and how it is connected to functional programming.

Functional-Reactive Programming

In the previous chapters, we learned about the functional programming paradigm. We explored the main functional programming concepts, techniques, and patterns. In this chapter, we are going to learn about the functional-reactive programming paradigm, including the following topics:

- Reactive programming
- Functional-reactive programming
- Streams
- Observables
- The observer pattern
- The iterator pattern
- Operators

We are going to learn what functional-reactive programming is and how it can help us to develop applications that are easier to extend and maintain.

Reactive programming

In this section, we are going to learn what the main differences are between functional programming and reactive programming as well as what principal benefits of reactive programming.

Functional programming versus functional-reactive programming

Functional programming and reactive programming should be considered as two different paradigms. Functional programming focuses on the interpretation of functions as mathematical functions—stateless and without side effects. On the other hand, reactive programming focuses on the propagation of changes as streams of events. The term *functional-reactive programming* is used to refer to a superset of reactive programming. Functional-reactive programming tries to take advantage of both the functional and reactive programming paradigms. For example, in functional-reactive programming, the event streams can be composed, we are encouraged to avoid external state mutations, and many of the functional programming principles are still relevant.

The benefits of functional-reactive programming

Functional-reactive programming is highly influenced by the functional programming principles and, as a result, many of the benefits of functional programming are also shared by functional-reactive programming. Functional-reactive applications are easier to reason about because they tend to avoid state mutations and side effects and promote a declarative style. They are particularly well suited for event-based architectures and concurrent systems. Functional-reactive programming is also considered by many developers a programming style that tends to be scalable because it follows the principle of composability.

Working with observables

Reactive programming requires us to change the way that we think about events in an application. Reactive programming requires us to think about events as a stream of values. For example, a mouse click event can be represented as a stream of data. Every click event generates a new value in the data stream. In reactive programming, we can use the stream of data to query and manipulate the values in the stream.

We are going to use the **Reactive Extensions Library for JavaScript (RxJS)**. RxJS provides us with an implementation of the observable pattern, as well as many operators and utilities that allow us to manipulate the observables. RxJS also includes helpers that allow us to create observables given different data types.

We can install RxJS using npm:

```
npm install rxjs
```

The observable pattern is also known as the **observable sequence pattern**, which is the result of putting two other popular patterns together: the observer and the iterator patterns. In this section, we are going to learn more about these patterns so that we can have a better understanding of what observables are and how they work internally.

The observer pattern

In an implementation of the observer pattern, we can have many known listener entities that subscribe to messages. The following code snippet contains a very basic implementation of a listener in the observer pattern:

```
class Listener<T> {

    public update: (message: T) => void;

    public constructor(fn: (message: T) => void) {
        this.update = fn;
    }

}
```

A Listener has a method named update, which is invoked when a second entity known as the Producer generates a new message. A Producer instance manages a number of Listener instances. A message can be generated with the notify method. The message is then passed to all the subscribed listeners. The following code snippet contains a very basic implementation of a producer in the observer pattern:

```
class Producer<T> {

    private _listeners: Listener<T>[] = [];

    public add(listener: Listener<T>) {
        this._listeners.push(listener);
    }

    public remove(listener: Listener<T>) {
        this._listeners = this._listeners.filter(
            l => l !== listener
        );
    }
```

```
    public notify(message: T) {
        this._listeners.forEach(
            l => l.update(message)
        );
    }

}
```

The following code snippet declares a couple of `Listener` instances and a `Producer` instance. It then subscribes both listeners to the `Producer` messages using the `add` method. Later, we use the `notify` method in `Producer` to send a message. The message will be received by all the subscribed listeners. In this case, both listeners will receive the message:

```
const listerner1 = new Listener(
    (msg: string) => console.log(`Listener 1: ${msg}`)
);

const listerner2 = new Listener(
    (msg: string) => console.log(`Listener 2: ${msg}`)
);

const notify = new Producer<string>();
notify.add(listerner1);
notify.add(listerner2);
notify.notify("Hello World!");
```

Now that we have learned how to implement the observer pattern, we are going to focus on the second pattern used by the observable sequence pattern—the iterator pattern.

The iterator pattern

To understand how the observable sequence pattern works, we also need to understand the iterator pattern. The following code snippet uses a generator to create an iterator that iterates the multiples of a given number in an array. Only the elements in the array that are multiples of a given number are iterated:

```
function* iterateOnMultiples(arr: number[], divisor: number) {
    for (let item of arr) {
        if (item % divisor === 0) {
            yield item;
        }
    }
}
```

To get an instance of the iterator, we only need to invoke the function and pass an array and a number as its arguments. The function returns an iterator that will return the numbers in the array that are multiples of the given number: 3. We can invoke the iterator's `next` method to get the next element. Each element has a property named `done` and a property named `value`. The `done` property can be used to check whether there are more items to be iterated. The `value` property can be used to access the value of the current item:

```
const iterator1 = iterateOnMultiples([1, 2, 3, 4, 5, 6, 7, 8, 9, 10], 3);

const iteratorResult1 = iterator1.next();
console.log(iteratorResult1.value);

if (iteratorResult1.done === false) {

    const iteratorResult2 = iterator1.next();
    console.log(iteratorResult2.value);

}
```

We can also iterate all the items in an iterator using a `for...of` statement, as opposed to accessing the `done` property by hand:

```
const iterator2 = iterateOnMultiples([1, 2, 3, 4, 5, 6, 7, 8, 9, 10], 3);

for (let value of iterator2) {
    console.log(value);
}
```

The observer and the iterator pattern can be very useful in many different scenarios. We can combine these two patterns in a pattern known as the **observable sequence**, or simply **observable**. An observable allows us to iterate and be notified about changes in a sequence. Now that we understand what is an observable is, we are going to learn how we can create instances of observables with RxJS.

Creating observables

Observables are streams of data, and this explains why it is easy to imagine that we can represent an event such as an `onClick` event using an observable. However, the use cases for observables are much more diverse than that. In this section, we are going to explore how to create an observable given different types.

Creating observables from a value

We can create an observable given a value using the `of` function. In the old versions of RxJS, the function `of` was a static method of the `Observable` class, which was available as `Observable.of`. This should remind us to use the `of` method of the `Applicative` type in category theory because observables take some inspiration from category theory. However, in RxJS 6.0, the `of` method is available as a standalone factory function:

```
import { of } from "rxjs";

const observable = of(1);

const subscription = observable.subscribe(
    (value) => console.log(value),
    (error: any) => console.log(error),
    () => console.log("Done!")
);

subscription.unsubscribe();
```

The preceding code snippet declares an observable with one unique value using the `of` function. The code snippet also showcases how we can subscribe to an observable using the `subscribe` method. The `subscribe` method takes three function arguments:

- **Item handler**: Invoked once for each item in the sequence.
- **Error handler**: Invoked if there is an error in the sequence. This argument is optional.
- **Done handler**: Invoked when there are no more items in the sequence. This argument is optional.

The following diagram is known as a **marble diagram**, and is used to represent observables in a visual manner. The arrow represents the time and the circles are values. In this case, we have only one value:

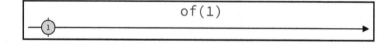

As we can see, the circle also has a small vertical line in the middle. This line is used to represent the last element in an observable. In this case, the item handler in the subscription will only be invoked once.

Creating observables from arrays

We can create an observable given an existing array using the `from` function:

```
import { from } from "rxjs";

const observable = from([10, 20, 30]);

const subscription = observable.subscribe(
    (value) => console.log(value),
    (error: any) => console.log(error),
    () => console.log("Done!")
);

subscription.unsubscribe();
```

The preceding code snippet declares an observable with three values using the `from` function. The code snippet also showcases how we can subscribe once more.

The following marble diagram represents the preceding example in a visual manner. The generated observable has three values (**10, 20,** and **30**) and **30** is the last element in the observable:

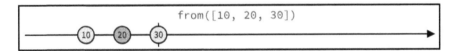

We can alternatively use the `interval` function to generate an array with a given number of elements:

```
import { interval } from "rxjs";

const observable = interval(10);

const subscription = observable.subscribe(
    (value) => console.log(value),
    (error: any) => console.log(error),
    () => console.log("Done!")
);

subscription.unsubscribe();
```

The preceding code snippet declares an observable with ten values using the `interval` function. The code snippet also showcases how we can subscribe once more. In this case, the item handler in the subscription will be invoked ten times.

The following marble diagram represents the preceding example in a visual manner. The generating observable has ten values, and 9 is the last item contained by it:

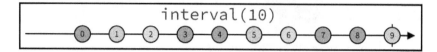

In this case, the item handler in the subscription will be invoked ten times.

Creating observables from events

It is also possible to create an observable using an event as the source of the items in the stream. We can do this using the fromEvent function:

```
import { fromEvent } from "rxjs";

const observable = fromEvent(document, "click");

const subscription = observable.subscribe(
    (value) => console.log(value)
);

subscription.unsubscribe();
```

In this case, the item handler in the subscription will be invoked as many times as the click event takes place.

 Please note that the preceding example can only be executed in a web browser. To execute the preceding code in a web browser, you will need to use a module bundler, such as Webpack. We will not cover this topic, since it is beyond the scope of this book.

Creating observables from callbacks

It is also possible to create an observable that will iterate the arguments of a callback using the bindCallback function:

```
import { bindCallback } from "rxjs";
import fetch from "node-fetch";

function getJSON(url: string, cb: (response: unknown|null) => void) {
    fetch(url)
        .then(response => response.json())
```

```
        .then(json => cb(json))
        .catch(_ => cb(null));
}

const uri = "https://jsonplaceholder.typicode.com/todos/1";
const observableFactory = bindCallback(getJSON);
const observable = observableFactory(uri);

const subscription = observable.subscribe(
    (value) => console.log(value)
);

subscription.unsubscribe();
```

The preceding example uses the `node-fetch` module because the fetch function is not available in Node.js. You can install the `node-fetch` module using the following npm command:

npm install node-fetch @types/node-fetch

The `getJSON` function takes a URL and a callback as its arguments. When we pass it to the `bindCallback` function, a new function is returned. The new function takes a URL as its only argument and returns an observable instead of taking a callback.

In Node.js, callbacks follow a well-defined pattern. The Node.js callbacks take two arguments, `error` and `result`, and don't throw exceptions. We must use the `error` argument to check whether something went wrong instead of a `try/catch` statement. RxJS also defines a function named `bindNodeCallback` that allows us to work with the callbacks:

```
import { bindNodeCallback } from "rxjs";
import * as fs from "fs";

const observableFactory = bindNodeCallback(fs.readFile);
const observable = observableFactory("./roadNames.txt");

const subscription = observable.subscribe(
    (value) => console.log(value.toString())
);

subscription.unsubscribe();
```

The helpers, `bindCallback` and `bindNodeCallback`, have very similar behavior, but the second has been specially designed to work with Node.js callbacks.

Creating observables from promises

Another potential source of items for an observable sequence is a `Promise`. RxJS also allows us to handle this use case with the `from` function. We must pass a `Promise` instance to the `from` function. In the following example, we use the `fetch` function to send an HTTP request. The `fetch` function returns a promise that is passed to the `from` function:

```
import { bindCallback } from "rxjs";
import fetch from "node-fetch";

const uri = "https://jsonplaceholder.typicode.com/todos/1";
const observable = from(fetch(uri)).pipe(map(x => x.json()));

const subscription = observable.subscribe(
  (value) => console.log(value.toString())
);

subscription.unsubscribe();
```

The generated observable will contain the result of the promise as its only item.

Cold and hot observables

The official RxJS documentation explores the differences between cold and hot observables as follows:

> *"Cold observables start running upon subscription, that is, the observable sequence only starts pushing values to the observers when Subscribe is called. Values are also not shared among subscribers. This is different from hot observables, such as mouse move events or stock tickers, which are already producing values even before a subscription is active. When an observer subscribes to a hot observable sequence, it will get all values in the stream that are emitted after it subscribes. The hot observable sequence is shared among all subscribers, and each subscriber is pushed the next value in the sequence."*

It is important to understand these differences if we want to have control over the execution flow of our components. The key point to remember is that cold observables are lazily evaluated.

Working with operators

In this section, we are going to learn how to use some functions known as operators, which allow us to manipulate observables in many different ways.

Pipe

In RxJS, observables have a method named `pipe`, which is very similar to the pipe operator in functional programming. When we pipe two functions, we generate a new function that passes the return of the first function as arguments to the second function in the pipe.

The idea is very similar in reactive programming. When we pipe an observable through an operator, we generate a new observable. The new observable passes each of the items in the original observable to an operator that transforms them into the items in the new sequence.

We are not going to include a code example here, because we are going to use the pipe method multiple times during the remaining part of this chapter.

Max

The `max` operator function can be used to find the biggest value in an observable. We must apply the `max` operator using the `pipe` method:

```
import { from } from "rxjs";
import { max } from "rxjs/operators";

const observable = from<number>([2, 30, 22, 5, 60, 1]);

observable.pipe(max());

const subscription = observable.subscribe(
    (value) => console.log(value)
);

subscription.unsubscribe();
```

The following marble diagram showcases the initial sequence and the result sequence after applying the `max` operator:

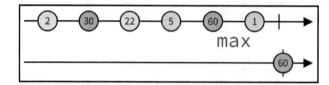

The result sequence contains only one value (the biggest value in the original sequence).

Every

The `every` operator function can be used to test whether all the values in an observable adhere to a given requirement:

```
import { from } from "rxjs";
import { every } from "rxjs/operators";

const observable = from<number>([1,2, 3, 4, 5]);

observable.pipe(every(x => x < 10));

const subscription = observable.subscribe(
    (value) => console.log(value)
);

subscription.unsubscribe();
```

The preceding code snippet uses the `every` operator to test that all the values in an observable are lower than ten. The following marble diagram showcases the initial sequence and the result sequence after applying the `every` operator:

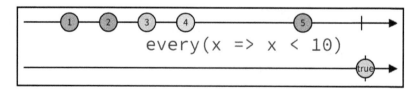

The result sequence contains only one value (true or false).

Find

The `find` operator function can be used to find the first value in an observable that adheres to a given constraint:

```
import { from } from "rxjs";
import { find } from "rxjs/operators";

const observable = from<number>([2, 30, 22, 5, 60, 1]);

observable.pipe(find(x => x > 10));

const subscription = observable.subscribe(
    (value) => console.log(value)
);

subscription.unsubscribe();
```

The preceding code snippet uses the `find` operator to find the first value in an observable greater than ten. The following marble diagram showcases the initial sequence and the result sequence after applying the `find` operator:

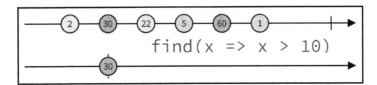

The result sequence contains only one value (the first value in the stream that matches the given constraint).

Filter

The `filter` operator function can be used to find the values in an observable that adhere to a given constraint:

```
import { from } from "rxjs";
import { filter } from "rxjs/operators";

const observable = from<number>([2, 30, 22, 5, 60, 1]);

observable.pipe(filter(x => x > 10));

const subscription = observable.subscribe(
```

```
    (value) => console.log(value)
);

subscription.unsubscribe();
```

The preceding code snippet uses the `filter` operator to find the values in an observable greater than ten. The following marble diagram showcases the initial sequence and the result sequence after applying the `filter` operator:

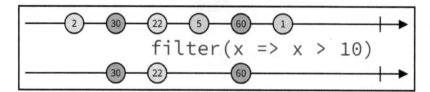

The result sequence contains only some values (the values in the stream that match the given constraint).

Map

The `map` operator function can be used to transform the values in an observable into derived values:

```
import { from } from "rxjs";
import { map } from "rxjs/operators";

const observable = from<number>([1, 2, 3]);

observable.pipe(map(x => 10 * x));

const subscription = observable.subscribe(
  (value) => console.log(value)
);

subscription.unsubscribe();
```

The preceding code snippet uses the `map` operator to transform the values in an observable into new values (the original value multiplied by ten). The following marble diagram showcases the initial sequence and the result sequence after applying the `map` operator:

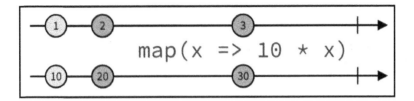

The result sequence contains a new mapped value for each value in the original sequence.

Reduce

The reduce operator function can be used to transform all the values in an observable into one single value:

```
import { from } from "rxjs";
import { reduce } from "rxjs/operators";

const observable = from<number>([1, 2, 3, 3, 4, 5]);

observable.pipe(reduce((x, y) => x + y));

const subscription = observable.subscribe(
    (value) => console.log(value)
);

subscription.unsubscribe();
```

The preceding code snippet uses the reduce operator to transform the values in an observable into a new single value (the total of all the values). The function that transforms multiple values into one single value is known as an accumulator. The following marble diagram showcases the initial sequence and the result sequence after applying the reduce operator:

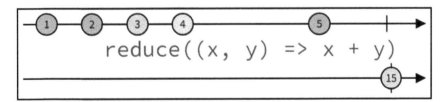

The result sequence contains only one value (the result of the accumulator).

Throttle

The `throttle` operator function can be used to reduce the number of values that are added to an observable:

```
import { fromEvent, interval } from "rxjs";
import { throttle, mapTo, scan } from "rxjs/operators";

const observable = fromEvent(document, "click")
                    .pipe(mapTo(1))
                    .pipe(throttle(x => interval(100)))
                    .pipe(scan((acc, one) => acc + one, 0));

const subscription = observable.subscribe(
    (value) => console.log(value)
);

subscription.unsubscribe();
```

The preceding code snippet creates an observable for `click` events. Every click will add an item to the sequence. The example also uses the `pipe` method and the `mapTo` function to map all the click events to the numeric value `1`. It is then when we use the `throttle` operator to reduce the number of values that are added to the sequence. If two or more click events take place within a time interval lower than the one declared by the interval, only the first value will be added to the sequence.

 Please note that the preceding example can only be executed in a web browser. To execute the preceding code in a web browser, you will need to use a module bundler such as Webpack. We will not cover this topic because it is beyond the scope of this book.

The following marble diagram showcases the initial sequence and the result sequence after applying the `reduce` operator:

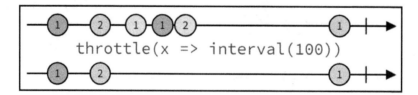

The result sequence only contains some values because the values that take place too close in time are ignored.

Merge

The `merge` operator function can be used to merge the values of two observables into value pairs:

```
import { from } from "rxjs";
import { merge } from "rxjs/operators";

const observableA = from<number>([20, 40, 60, 80, 100]);
const observableB = from<number>([1, 1]);

const observableC = observableA.pipe(merge<number, number>(observableB));

const subscription = observableC.subscribe(
    (value) => console.log(value)
);

subscription.unsubscribe();
```

The preceding code snippet uses the `merge` operator to combine the values of two observables into a new observable. The values are ordered chronologically. The following marble diagram showcases the initial sequences and the result sequence after applying the `merge` operator:

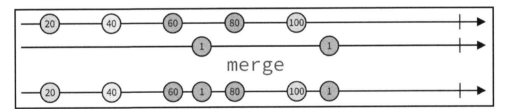

The result sequence contains the values of both observables ordered in the same sequence as they took place in time.

Zip

The `zip` operator function can be used to merge the values of two observables into value pairs:

```
import { from } from "rxjs";
import { zip } from "rxjs/operators";

const observableA = from<number>([1, 2, 3, 3, 4, 5]);
```

```
const observableB = from<string>(["A", "B", "C", "D"]);

const observableC = observableA.pipe(zip<number, string>(observableB));

const subscription = observableC.subscribe(
    (value) => console.log(value)
);

subscription.unsubscribe();
```

The preceding code snippet uses the `zip` operator to combine the values of two observables into a new observable. The values in the new observable are value pairs that contain a value from the first observable and a value from the second observable and are grouped by their index in the sequence. The following marble diagram showcases the initial sequences and the result sequence after applying the `zip` operator:

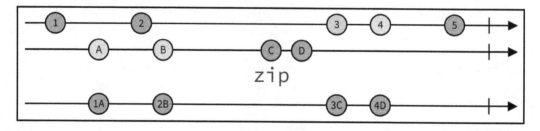

The result sequence contains the values of both observables merged into single value pairs.

Summary

In this chapter, we have learned about the functional-reactive programming paradigm. We have learned that many of the functional programming ideas, such as pure functions and function composition, can be applied to reactive programming. We also learned what observables are and how we can create them and work with them.

In the next chapter, we are going to learn about some production-ready functional programming libraries, such as Ramda and Immutable.js.

10
Real-World Functional Programming

In the preceding chapter of this book, we have learned about functional programming and functional reactive programming. We tried to avoid using external libraries, because our main goal was to understand the techniques, patterns, and principles of the functional programming and functional-reactive programming paradigms.

In this chapter, we are going to learn about the following topics:

- Composing with Ramda
- Currying and partial application with Ramda
- Lenses with Ramda
- Working with Immutable.js
- Working with Immer
- Working with Funfix

We are going to revisit once more some of the main concepts that we have explored throughout this book. However, this time, our focus will not be to understand these concepts (it is assumed that we already do). Instead, we are going to focus on the usage of some production-ready functional programming libraries, such as Ramda or Immutable.js.

Working with Ramda

Ramda is an open source functional programming library that which includes many utility functions that can help us to put some of the main functional programming techniques into practice. Ramda can be compared to other libraries, such as Lodash or Underscore. However, the Ramda API is much more influenced by the functional programming principle than these other libraries. For example, Ramda has been designed in a way that makes composability and immutability two of the main characteristics of its components.

We can install Ramda using the following **npm** command:

```
npm install ramda @types/ramda
```

In the following sections, we are going to learn how to use Ramda to implement function compositions and lenses.

Composition

In the previous chapters, we declared a higher-order function named compose, which allows us to compose two functions:

```
const compose = <T>(f: (x: T) => T, g: (x: T) => T) => (x: T) => f(g(x));
```

The compose function allowed us to demonstrate how function composition works, but it had some limitations. For example, the compose function only takes one generic type, parameter T, which means that we can only compose two unary functions, f and g, that take one argument of type T:

```
const trim = (s: string) => s.trim();
const capitalize = (s: string) => s.toUpperCase();
const trimAndCapitalize = compose(trim, capitalize);
const result = trimAndCapitalize(" hello world ");
console.log(result); // "HELLO WORLD"
```

In a real-world application, we may need to compose two functions f and g that take an argument of two different types T1 and T2. The following code snippet uses the compose function from Ramda instead of the one that we declared previously:

```
import R from "ramda";

const trim = (s: string) => s.trim();
const capitalize = (s: string) => s.toUpperCase();
const trimAndCapitalize = R.compose(trim, capitalize);
const result = trimAndCapitalize(" hello world ");
console.log(result); // "HELLO WORLD"
```

The compose function from Ramda is a much better alternative for real-world applications because it has been used in hundreds of projects and tested with thousands of functions.

Partial application and currying

We have also learned that the functional composition only works with unary functions and that if we wish to compose functions, that are not unary, such as binary functions we can use function partial application to invoke one of the function with only some of its arguments and generate new functions that take the remaining arguments. Finally, we also learned that we can use currying to transform a given function into a function that can be partially applied:

```
function curry3<T1, T2, T3, T4>(fn: (a: T1, b: T2, c: T3) => T4) {
    return (a: T1) => (b: T2) => (c: T3) => fn(a, b, c);
}

const trim = (s: string) => s.trim();
const capitalize = (s: string) => s.toUpperCase();
const trimAndCapitalize = R.compose(trim, capitalize);
const replace = (s: string, f: string, r: string) => s.split(f).join(r);

const curriedReplace = curry3(replace);

const trimCapitalizeAndReplace = compose(
    trimAndCapitalize,
    curriedReplace("/")("-")
);

const result = trimCapitalizeAndReplace(" 13/feb/1989 ");
console.log(result); // "13-FEB-1989"
```

The preceding code snippet uses the `curry3` function to transform a ternary function into a function that can be partially applied. Again, in a real-world application, it is not recommended to create a custom implementation, and we should try to use a battle-tested library instead. Fortunately, we are not going to need to search around for very long because Ramda includes a function named `curry` that can be used to achieve just what we want:

```
import R from "ramda";

const trim = (s: string) => s.trim();
const capitalize = (s: string) => s.toUpperCase();
const replace = (s: string, f: string, r: string) => s.split(f).join(r);

const trimCapitalizeAndReplace = R.compose(
 R.compose(trim, capitalize),
 R.curry(replace)("/")("-")
);

const result = trimCapitalizeAndReplace(" 13/feb/1989 ");
console.log(result); // "13-FEB-1989"
```

The preceding code snippet declares three functions in a way that is completely agnostic of Ramda. We then use the Ramda utility functions, `compose` and `curry`, to generate a new function named `trimCapitalizeAndReplace`.

Lenses

We learned about lenses in some of the previous chapters. In one of the last examples, we implemented lenses in a way that is very close to the implementation provided by Ramda.

We implemented a higher-order function named `lens` that can be used to create a `Lens` implementation. The `lens` function takes two functions that must implement the `Prop` and `Assoc` interfaces:

```
interface Lens<T1, T2> {
    get(o: T1): T2;
    set(o: T2, v: T1): T1;
}

type Prop<T, K extends keyof T> = (o: T) => T[K];
type Assoc<T, K extends keyof T> = (v: T[K], o: T) => T;

const lens = <T1, K extends keyof T1>(
    getter: Prop<T1, K>,
```

```
        setter: Assoc<T1, K>,
): Lens<T1, T1[K]> => {
    return {
        get: (obj: T1) => getter(obj),
        set: (val: T1[K], obj: T1) => setter(val, obj),
    };
}

const view = <T1, T2>(lens: Lens<T1, T2>, obj: T1) => lens.get(obj);

const set = <T1, K extends keyof T1>(
    lens: Lens<T1, T1[K]>,
    val: T1[K],
    obj: T1
) => lens.set(val, obj);
```

We can then create a Lens implementation passing the Assoc and Prop implementations to the Lens function:

```
class Street {

    public readonly num: number;
    public readonly name: string;

    public constructor(num: number, name: string) {
        this.num = num;
        this.name = name;
    }

}

class Address {

    public readonly city: string;
    public readonly street: Street;

    public constructor(city: string, street: Street) {
        this.city = city;
        this.street = street;
    }

}

const propStreet: Prop<Address, "street"> = (o: Address) => o.street;

const assocStreet: Assoc<Address, "street"> = (v: Address["street"], o:
Address) => {
    return new Address(o.city, v);
```

```
};

const streetLens = lens(propStreet, assocStreet);
```

Once we have a `Lens` instance, we can use the `set` and `view` functions to `read` and `set` the value of a property in an immutable object:

```
const address = new Address(
    "London",
    new Street(1, "rathbone square")
);

const street = view(streetLens, address);

const address2 = set(
    streetLens,
    new Street(
        address.street.num,
        R.toUpper(address.street.name)
    ),
    address
);
```

Now that we know the basics about Ramda, we can implement the preceding code snippet once more using some of its utility functions. Ramda includes the following utility functions, among others:

- The `prop` function allows us to declare a property getter. It expects the name of a property as an argument.
- The `assoc` function allows us to declare a property setter. It expects the name of a property as an argument.
- The `lens` function allows us to declare a lens instance. It expects a property getter (`prop`) and setter (`assoc`) as arguments.
- The `lensProp` function allows us to declare a lens instance. It expects the name of a property as an argument.
- The `view` function allows us to get the value of a property in an object. It expects a lens instance and an object as arguments.
- The `set` function allows us to set the value of a property in an object. It expects a lens instance, a new value, and an object as arguments.

In the following code snippet, we use the `lensProp`, `view`, and `set` functions:

```
import R from "ramda";

class Street {

    public readonly num: number;
    public readonly name: string;

    public constructor(num: number, name: string) {
        this.num = num;
        this.name = name;
    }

}

class Address {

    public readonly city: string;
    public readonly street: Street;

    public constructor(city: string, street: Street) {
        this.city = city;
        this.street = street;
    }

}

const streetLens = R.lensProp("street");

const address = new Address(
    "London",
    new Street(1, "rathbone square")
);

const street = R.view<Address, Street>(streetLens, address);

const address2 = R.set<Address, Street>(
    streetLens,
    new Street(
        address.street.num,
        R.toUpper(address.street.name)
    ),
    address
);
```

Use of the `prop` and `assoc` functions are not required in most cases thanks to the `lensProp` instead of the `lens` function.

Working with Immutable.js

In the preceding chapters, we also learned about immutability and the benefits of using immutable data objects. We learned that we can use the `readonly` keyword to declare immutable objects:

```
class Street {

    public readonly num: number;
    public readonly name: string;

    public constructor(num: number, name: string) {
        this.num = num;
        this.name = name;
    }

}

class Address {

    public readonly city: string;
    public readonly street: Street;

    public constructor(city: string, street: Street) {
        this.city = city;
        this.street = street;
    }

}
```

We also learned that working with immutable objects can sometimes be very verbose and tedious and that lenses can help us to overcome these difficulties. We are now going to learn about a library that can help us to declare immutable objects. The library is known as **Immutable.js**, and it also includes an API similar tot he lenses API. We can install Immutable.js using the following command:

```
npm install immutable
```

We can define type-safe immutable classes with Immutable.js, using the `Record` type as follows:

```
import { Record } from "immutable";

interface StreetInterface {
    num: number;
    name: string;
}
```

```
const StreetRecord = Record({
    num: 0,
    name: ""
});

class Street extends StreetRecord implements StreetInterface {
    constructor(props: StreetInterface) {
        super(props);
    }
}
```

We are going to define one more immutable class named Address. The Address class contains an instance of the Street class:

```
interface AddressInterface {
    city: string;
    street: Street;
}

const AddressRecord = Record({
    city: "",
    street: new Street({
        num: 0,
        name: ""
    })
});

class Address extends AddressRecord implements AddressInterface {
    constructor(props: AddressInterface) {
        super(props);
    }
}
```

To create an instance of an immutable class, we need to pass all the required properties as a plain object:

```
const address = new Address({
    city: "Lonson",
    street: new Street({
        num: 1,
        name: "rathbone square"
    })
});
```

When we declare an immutable class with Immutable.js, the class inherits some methods that behave like a lens. We can use the `get` method to get the value of a property and the `set` method to create a new immutable instance using an updated value:

```
const street = address.get("street");
const street2 = street.set("name", "Rathbone square");
const address2 = address.set("street", street2);

console.log(
    address.toJS(),
    address2.toJS()
);
```

Declaring an immutable class with Immutable.js is more tedious than declaring them with the `readonly` access modifier, but we get lenses as a built-in feature in exchange for our effort.

Working with Immer

We are going to take a look at another popular immutability library. The library is known as **Immer**, and it can be installed using the following npm command:

```
npm install immer
```

Immer allows us to define immutable classes using the `readonly` access modifier. This means that we can also create instances of our classes using a standard class constructor:

```
import produce from "immer";

class Street {

    public readonly num: number;
    public readonly name: string;

    public constructor(num: number, name: string) {
        this.num = num;
        this.name = name;
    }

}

class Address {

    public readonly city: string;
    public readonly street: Street;
```

```
    public constructor(city: string, street: Street) {
        this.city = city;
        this.street = street;
    }

}

const address = new Address(
    "London",
    new Street(1, "rathbone square")
);
```

Immer can generate a new version of an immutable object using a method named produce. The produce function takes the current version of an immutable object as its first argument. The second argument is a callback function that takes one argument known as the draft state. The draft state is a mutable version of the initial version and, within the callback function, we can mutate it as much as we want:

```
const address2 = produce(address, draftAddress => {
    draftAddress.street.name = "Rathbone square";
});
```

The produce function returns a new immutable object without mutating the original object. The Immer API can be considered superior to the Immutable.js API, because it imposes fewer constraints in our class declarations and constructors. Immer is not based on lenses and allows us to work with immutable objects using an innovative approach that utilizes proxies internally.

Working with Funfix

Funfix is a collection of functional programming utility functions. Funfix can be compared with Ramda. Just like Ramda, Funfix can be used to compose functions or partially apply functions. However, in this section, we are going to focus on the usage of some of the Funfix features that are related to some of the data types that we previously explored in Chapter 7, *Category Theory*.

We are going to start by installing Funfix:

```
npm install funfix @types/funfix
```

The examples that we are going to implement in this section are going to require a couple of additional npm modules. We are going to use `node-fetch` to send HTTP requests from a Node.js application. We are also going to use some of the Node.js core modules, which means that we are going to need the type definitions for Node.js as well:

```
npm install node-fetch @type/node-fetch @types/node
```

In our first Funfix example, we are going to define a monad named `argsIO` using the `IO.of` factory method. As we learned in the previous chapters, a monad is a functor, and a functor is a container. In this case, the container contains a function that performs an I/O operation: reading the command-line arguments (`process.argv`). The `IO` type is used to store a function that describes some computation with side effects, such as reading some data from a file or mutating the elements in the **Document Object Model (DOM)**. Describing actions in this way allows for `IO` instances to be composed and passed around, while keeping functions pure and maintaining referential transparency.

We are also going to declare two functions named `readFile` and `stdoutWrite`. Both of these functions return a monad instance, and both monads contain I/O operations. The first one reads a file from the filesystem, and the second one prints some information in the standard output:

```
import * as R from "ramda";
import * as fs from "fs";
import { IO } from "funfix";

const argsIO = IO.of(() => R.tail(R.tail(process.argv))[0]);
const readFile = (filename: string) => IO.of(() =>
fs.readFileSync(filename, "utf8"));
const stdoutWrite = (data: string) => IO.of(() =>
process.stdout.write(data));

const loudCat = argsIO.chain(readFile)
    .map(R.toUpper)
    .chain(stdoutWrite);

try {
    loudCat.run();
} catch(e) {
    console.log(e);
}
```

The preceding code snippet also declares a monad named `loudCat` using the `chain` method to pass the command line arguments to the file reading operation and the `map` method to transform the file contents into upper case. Finally, it uses the `chain` method one last time to pass the uppercase text to the standard output.

One of the main characteristics of monads in Funfix is that they are lazily evaluated, and all of the preceding operations don't take place until we invoke the `run` method. If everything goes well, we can pass the name of a file using the command-line interface:

```
node example.js test.txt
```

The uppercase contents of the file should be displayed on the standard output. The following example uses the `node-fetch` module to send an HTTP request. The function that performs the HTTP request is contained by a monad. This time, the monad is not created by the `IO.of` factory function because it is created with the `IO.async` factory function instead. We use the `IO.async` factory function because it is required by Funfix when an asynchronous operation is wrapped by a monad. The example also uses the `Either` type, which is another Functor and monad. It can be used to wrap a value that can be of two possible values:

```
import { IO, Success, Failure, Either, Left, Right } from "funfix";
import fetch from "node-fetch";

interface Todo {
    userId: number;
    id: number;
    title: string;
    completed: boolean;
}

const getTodos = IO.async<Either<Error, Todo[]>>((ec, cb) => {
    fetch(
        "https://jsonplaceholder.typicode.com/todos"
    ).then(response => {
        return response.json().then(
            (json: Todo[]) => cb(Success(Right(json)))
        )
    })
    .catch(err => cb(Failure(Left(err)))));
});

const logTodos = getTodos.map((either) => {
    return either.map(todos => todos.map(t => console.log(t.title)));
});

logTodos.run();
```

The error-handling logic is very simple because the `map` method of the `Either` type only maps the values when the type of its value is not an error. Just as before, the entire logic is lazily evaluated and nothing really happens until we invoke the `run` method in the `logTodos` monad.

Summary

In this chapter, we have learned how to use some real-world functional programming libraries, including Ramda, Fundix, Immer, and Immutable.js. Throughout this book, we have learned about the main characteristics, principles, patterns, and principles of the functional programming and functional-reactive programming paradigm. These concepts provide you with a set of powerful tools that will help you to useapplications that are easier to reason about, more testable, and easier to maintain.

I hope that you enjoy this book and that you are eager to continue your functional programming-learning journey. In the appendices, you will find a guide that can be used to discover new functional libraries and additional functional programming concepts that you can explore on your own if you wish to learn more.

Functional Programming Learning Road Map

The following guide can be used to track our level of knowledge regarding functional programming. This guide was developed for the *Fantasyland* institute of learning for the *LambdaConf* conference. It was designed for statically-typed functional programming languages that implement category theory.

 Languages such as Haskell support category theory natively, but, as we learned previously, we can take advantage of category theory in TypeScript by implementing it or using some third-party libraries. Not all the items in the list are 100% applicable to TypeScript due to language differences, but most of them are 100% applicable.

Beginner

To reach the *beginner* level, you will need to master the following concepts and skills:

CONCEPTS	SKILLS
• Immutable data • Second-order functions • Constructoring and destructuring • Function composition • First-class functions and lambdas	• Use second-order functions (`map`, `filter`, `fold`) on immutable data structures • Destructure values to access their components • Use data types to represent optionality • Read basic type signatures • Pass lambdas to second-order functions

Advanced beginner

To reach the *advanced beginner* level, you will need to master the following concepts and skills:

CONCEPTS	SKILLS
• Algebraic data types • Pattern matching • Parametric polymorphism • General recursion • Type classes, instances, and laws • Lower-order abstractions (equal, semigroup, monoid, and so on) • Referential transparency and totality • Higher-order functions • Partial application, currying, and point-free style	• Solve problems without nulls, exceptions, or type casts • Process and transform recursive data structures using recursion • Able to use functional programming *in the small* • Write basic monadic code for a concrete monad • Create type class instances for custom data types • Model a business domain with **abstract data types** (**ADTs**) • Write functions that take and return functions • Reliably identify and isolate pure code from impure code • Avoid introducing unnecessary lambdas and named parameters

Intermediate

To reach the *intermediate* level, you will need to master the following concepts and skills:

CONCEPTS	SKILLS
• Generalized algebraic data type • Higher-kinded types • Rank-N types • Folds and unfolds • Higher-order abstractions (category, functor, monad) • Basic optics • Implement efficient persistent data structures • Existential types • Embedded DSLs using combinators	• Able to implement large functional programming applications • Test code using generators and properties • Write imperative code in a purely functional way through monads • Use popular purely functional libraries to solve business problems • Separate decision from effects • Write a simple custom lawful monad • Write production medium-sized projects • Use lenses and prisms to manipulate data • Simplify types by hiding irrelevant data with existential

Proficient

To reach the *proficient* level, you will need to master the following concepts and skills:

CONCEPTS	SKILLS
• Codata • (Co)recursion schemes • Advanced optics • Dual abstractions (comonad) • Monad transformers • Free monads and extensible effects • Functional architecture • Advanced functors (exponential, profunctors, contravariant) • Embedded **domain-specific languages (DSLs)** using **generalized algebraic datatypes (GADTs)** • Advanced monads (continuation, logic) • Type families, **functional dependencies (FDs)**	• Design a minimally powerful monad transformer stack • Write concurrent and streaming programs • Use purely functional mocking in tests. • Use type classes to modularly model different effects • Recognize type patterns and abstract over them • Use functional libraries in novel ways • Use optics to manipulate state • Write custom lawful monad transformers • Use free monads/extensible effects to separate concerns • Encode invariants at the type level. • Effectively use FDs/type families to create safer code

Expert

To reach the *expert* level, you will need to master the following concepts and skills:

CONCEPTS	SKILLS
• High performance • Kind polymorphism • Generic programming • Type-level programming • Dependent-types, singleton types • Category theory • Graph reduction • Higher-order abstract syntax • Compiler design for functional languages • Profunctor optics	• Design a generic, lawful library with broad appeal • Prove properties manually using equational reasoning • Design and implement a new functional programming language • Create novel abstractions with laws • Write distributed systems with certain guarantees • Use proof systems to formally prove properties of code • Create libraries that do not permit invalid states. • Use dependent typing to prove more properties at compile time • Understand deep relationships between different concepts • Profile, debug, and optimize purely functional code with minimal sacrifices

Summary

This guide should be a good resource to guide you in your future functional-programming learning efforts. In this book, we started without any previous knowledge of functional programming, and we have reached the *intermediate* level. Becoming an expert on functional programming will take some time, but at this point, we know enough about it to take advantage of its capabilities and enjoy its main benefits.

Directory of TypeScript Functional Programming Libraries

In this appendix, you will find a list of functional programming libraries compatible with TypeScript grouped according to the following categories:

- **Functional programming**: General-purpose functional programming utilities, including the `compose` function
- **Category theory**: Libraries that provide implementations of algebraic data types
- **Laziness**: Libraries that provide utilities for the implementation of lazy evaluation
- **Immutability**: Libraries that provide utilities for the implementation of immutable data structures
- **Optics**: Libraries that provide implementations of functional optics and lenses.
- **Functional-reactive programming**: General-purpose, functional-reactive programming utilities, such as observables
- **Others**: Libraries that do not focus on functional programming, but that are highly influenced by its principles

Functional programming

The following libraries allow us to take advantage of immutability in TypeScript:

Library	Description	Link
Ramda	A practical pure functional library for JavaScript programmers.	`https://github.com/ramda/ramda`
`fp-ts`	Pure functional programming utilities for TypeScript applications.	`https://github.com/gcanti/fp-ts`
Underscore	A collection of helper functions that includes some functional programming helpers.	`https://github.com/jashkenas/underscore`
Lodash	A collection of helper functions that includes some functional programming helpers.	`https://github.com/lodash/lodash`
`wu.js`	Higher-order functions for ES6 iterators.	`https://github.com/fitzgen/wu.js/`

Category theory

The following libraries allow us to take advantage of immutability in TypeScript:

Library	Description	Link
Ramda-fantasy	Algebraic data types compatible with the Fantasyland specification for easy integration with Ramda.js.	`https://github.com/ramda/ramda-fantasy`
`io-ts`	TypeScript-compatible, runtime-type system for IO decoding/encoding.	`https://github.com/gcanti/io-ts`
Funfix	Funfix is a library of type classes and data types for functional programming in JavaScript, TypeScript, and Flow.	`https://github.com/funfix/funfix`

Laziness

The following libraries allow us to take advantage of immutability in TypeScript:

Library	Description	Link
Lazy.js	Lazy.js is a functional utility library for JavaScript, similar to Underscore and Lodash, but with a lazy engine under the hood that strives to do as little work as possible, while being as flexible as possible.	https://github.com/dtao/lazy.js/
Transducers-js	A high-performance transducers implementation for JavaScript.	https://github.com/cognitect-labs/transducers-js

Immutability

The following libraries allow us to take advantage of immutability in TypeScript:

Library	Description	Link
Immutable.js	Immutable persistent data collections for Javascript that increase efficiency and simplicity.	https://github.com/facebook/immutable-js
Immer	Immer is a tiny package that allows you to work with immutable state in a more convenient way. It is based on the copy-on-write mechanism.	https://github.com/mweststrate/immer

Optics and lenses

The following libraries allow us to take advantage of immutability in TypeScript:

Library	Description	Link
monocle-ts	Functional optics: A (partial) porting of Scala monocle to TypeScript.	https://github.com/gcanti/monocle-ts
lens.ts	A TypeScript Lens implementation with property proxy.	https://github.com/utatti/lens.ts
Lenses	A small functional lens library for TypeScript with the goal of being small, with zero dependencies, and strong, precise types. It is inspired by Aether, for F#.	https://github.com/atomicobject/lenses
Lenticular.ts	An implementation of functional lenses in JavaScript/TypeScript.	https://github.com/tomasdeml/lenticular.ts

Functional-reactive programming

The following libraries allow us to take advantage of reactive programming in TypeScript:

Library	Description	Link
RxJS	A reactive programming library for JavaScript.	`https://github.com/ReactiveX/rxjs`
Xstream	An intuitive, small, and fast functional reactive stream library for JavaScript.	`https://github.com/x-stream/xstream`
`Bacon.js`	A small functional reactive programming lib for JavaScript.	`https://github.com/baconjs/bacon.js/`

Others

The following libraries allow us to take advantage of immutability in TypeScript:

Library	Description	Link
React	A library for the development of user interfaces that is highly influenced by functional programming principles.	`https://github.com/facebook/react`
Redux	Redux is a state container for JavaScript apps, and is highly influenced by functional programming principles.	`https://github.com/reduxjs/redux`
`Cycle.js`	A library for the development of user interfaces that is highly influenced by functional-reactive programming.	`https://github.com/cyclejs/cyclejs`
Mobx	A library for the development of user interfaces that is highly influenced by functional-reactive programming.	`https://github.com/mobxjs/mobx`

Summary

This appendix provides you with a quick reference of some popular functional programming and functional-reactive programming libraries. These libraries, together with the techniques and principles that we have learned previously in this book, should provide you with everything you need to create a number of real-world functional programming applications.

Other Books You May Enjoy

If you enjoyed this book, you may be interested in these other books by Packt:

Hands-On TypeScript for C# and .NET Core Developers
Francesco Abbruzzese

ISBN: 9781789130287

- Organize, test, and package large TypeScript code base
- Add TypeScript to projects using TypeScript declaration files
- Perform DOM manipulation with TypeScript
- Develop Angular projects with the Visual Studio Angular project template
- Define and use inheritance, abstract classes, and methods
- Leverage TypeScript-type compatibility rules
- Use WebPack to bundle JavaScript and other resources such as CSS to improve performance
- Build custom directives and attributes, and learn about animations

TypeScript 3.0 Quick Start Guide
Patrick Desjardins

ISBN: 9781789345575

- Set up the environment quickly to get started with TypeScript
- Configure TypeScript with essential configurations that run along your code
- Structure the code using Types and Interfaces to create objects
- Demonstrate how to create object-oriented code with TypeScript
- Abstract code with generics to make the code more reusable
- Transform the actual JavaScript code to be compatible with TypeScript

Leave a review - let other readers know what you think

Please share your thoughts on this book with others by leaving a review on the site that you bought it from. If you purchased the book from Amazon, please leave us an honest review on this book's Amazon page. This is vital so that other potential readers can see and use your unbiased opinion to make purchasing decisions, we can understand what our customers think about our products, and our authors can see your feedback on the title that they have worked with Packt to create. It will only take a few minutes of your time, but is valuable to other potential customers, our authors, and Packt. Thank you!

Index

A

algebraic data types 119
anonymous function 29, 30
apply method 80, 82
arity 23
arrow function
  using 52, 54
asynchronous flow control
  composite 61
  concurrent 60
  race 60
  series 61
  waterfall 61
asynchronous functions
  about 64
  async 64, 66
  await 64, 66
asynchronous generators 66
asynchronous iteration (for await...of) 67

B

bind method 80, 81
Browser Object Model (BOM) 72

C

call method 80, 82
callback hell 54
callback parameters
  covariant checking 61, 62
callbacks 51
category theory
  about 119, 121
  libraries, reference 186
closures
  about 96, 98
  private members 101, 103

static variables 98, 99, 101
currying 110, 111

D

declarative programming
  about 17
  versus imperative programming 17, 19
Document Object Model (DOM) 72, 178

E

event loop
  about 73, 75
  frames 74
  heap 75
  stack 75
every operator 160

F

filter operator 161
find operator 161
first-class citizens 21
frame 74
function arity 23
function declaration 31
function expressions 31
function parameters
  commas, trailing in function arguments 32
  default parameters 34
  optional parameters 33
  rest parameters 35, 38
  working with 32
function
  anonymous function 29
  named function 29
  overloading 38, 39
  scope 40, 43

types 28
functional composition 106
functional programming (FP)
  about 11
  benefits 10
  libraries, reference 186
  versus functional-reactive programming 150
functional programming techniques
  about 106, 114
  composition 106, 108
  currying 110
  partial application 108
  pattern matching 117
  pipe 113
  point-free style 114
  recursion 116
  strictBindCallApply 112
functional-reactive programming
  benefits 150
  libraries, reference 188
functions
  as first-class citizens 21
Functor
  Applicative 122
  characteristics 121
  Either 126, 128, 129
  Maybe 123, 125
  monads 129
Funfix
  working with 177, 180

G

garbage collection 40
generators 62

H

heap 75
higher-order functions 23, 51
hoisting 31, 42, 44

I

immediately-invoked function expression (IIFE) 44,
  46, 47, 87
Immer
  working with 176

immutability 19, 21
immutable data structure
  about 133, 135, 136
  libraries, reference 187
immutable.js file
  working with 174, 176
imperative programming
  versus declarative programming 17
implementation signature 38
input/output (I/O) operations 56
iterator 62
iterator pattern 152

L

Lambda expressions 22
Last-in-first-out (LIFO) 75
lazy evaluation 144, 147
lazy-evaluated APIs 25, 26
lenses 137, 138, 140
lexical scoping 41

M

map operator 162
marble diagram 154
max operator 159
merge operator 165

N

named function 29, 30

O

object prototype
  accessing 96
object-oriented programming (OOP) 9
observable sequence pattern 150, 153
observables
  cold observable 158
  creating 153
  creating, from arrays 155
  creating, from callbacks 156
  creating, from events 156
  creating, from promises 158
  creating, from value 154
  hot observable 158

iterator pattern 152
  observer pattern 151
  working with 150
observer pattern 151, 152
operators
  every 160
  filter 161
  find 161
  map 162
  max 159
  merge 165
  pipe 159
  reduce 163
  throttle 164
  working with 159
  zip 165
optics
  about 136
  lenses 137
  libraries, reference 187
  prism 141
  types 136
overload signatures 38

P

partial application 108, 109
pattern matching 117
pipe function 113
pipe operator 159
pipeline operator proposal
  reference 113
point-free style 114, 116
prisms 141, 143, 144
promise
  about 57, 58, 61
  fulfilled state 57
  pending state 57
  rejected state 57
property shadowing 94
prototype chain 94
prototypes
  about 85, 87
  inheritance 90, 93
  instance properties, versus class properties 87,
    89

pure functions
  about 12
  no side effects 13, 15

R

Ramda
  composition 168
  currying 169
  lenses, implementing 170, 172
  partial application 169
  working with 168
Reactive Extensions Library for JavaScript (RxJS)
  150
reactive programming 149
recursion 116
reduce operator 163
referential transparency 16
runtime environment
  setting up 72

S

specialized overloading signature 40
stack 75
STACK 73
stack overflow error 75
state changes (state mutations) 11
stateless code
  versus stateful code 16
strict mode
  reference 76
strictBindCallApply 112

T

Tacit programming 114
tag function 48
ternary function 23
this operator
  about 76
  in function context 77, 79
  in global context 77
throttle operator 164
TypeScript
  as functional programming language 10

V

variadic functions 23

Y

yield* expression

used, for delegating from one generator to another 68

Z

zip operator 165

CPSIA information can be obtained
at www.ICGtesting.com
Printed in the USA
JSHW061239160223
37729JS00003B/60